Managing Classroom

Neville Bennett

and

Elisabeth Dunne

STANLEY
THORNES

Text © Neville Bennett & Elisabeth Dunne 1992
Design and artwork © Simon & Schuster Education 1992

First published in 1992 in Great Britain by
Simon and Schuster Education

Published in 1994 by
Stanley Thornes (Publishers) Ltd
Ellenborough House
Wellington Street
CHELTENHAM GL50 1YW
England

96 97 98 99 00 / 10 9 8 7 6 5 4 3 2 1

A catalogue record for this book is available from the British Library.

ISBN 0 7487 2071 5

Typeset in $10\frac{1}{2}$ pt on 12 pt Sabon
by Photographics, Honiton, Devon
Printed in Great Britain by T. J. Press (Padstow) Ltd.

Contents

Acknowledgements

This book reports the findings of a study partly funded by the Leverhulme Trust. It could not have been written without the support and co-operation of a large number of people. Particular gratitude is expressed to the teachers with whom we have worked, and in whose classrooms we have carried out joint inquiries. It was they who had the courage to experiment and thereby to set up the conditions under which we could ascertain clearly issues central to the implementation of co-operative groups.

A special word of thanks is due to Cathie Holden. She laboured long over the analysis of transcripts, and carried out her own study into possible sex differences in co-operative groups, part of which is reported in Chapter 3.

Finally, thank you to Jo Small who undertook the onerous job of typing the drafts. This she did with characteristic speed and good humour.

1   Introduction

The 1990s herald a period of great change in the way we run our schools, and in the curriculum we 'deliver' or enact in our classrooms. The content of the primary curriculum will, of course, change in line with the requirements of the National Curriculum, but not necessarily the ways in which that content is taught. The originators of the National Curriculum specifically avoided making prescriptions about teaching styles or strategies, believing that these were areas of professional judgement best left to the teacher. We agree with this but believe it is important that these judgements are informed by current theories, ideas and research findings, particularly at a time when the theories which underpin current practices are seriously being questioned. Central to the current debate is the crucial question of how children learn, and the optimal conditions for their learning. This introductory chapter therefore considers first the question of how children learn, then discusses implications for classroom practice. Finally the material assesses, from recent research, the extent to which current practice is consistent with contemporary conceptions of learning.

How children learn

The topic of how children learn is a complex one, and no attempt is made here to provide a full and critical exposition. The aim of this section is to capture the essence of learning by identifying core issues, and by considering the ideas of the different theorists in the debate.

The first point to note is that what children learn in the classroom will depend to a large extent on what they already know. Irrespective of their age, children will have some knowledge and some conception of the classroom topic they are faced with, which they have acquired from books, television, talking to parents and friends, visits to places of interest, previous work in school, and so on. However, these conceptions, or schema as they are generally called, are likely to be incomplete, hazy or even plain wrong. They are, nevertheless, the children's current ideas, which they use to make sense of everyday experiences. In other words, children do not come to any lesson empty-headed; they come with partial schema. For example, a top junior teacher we observed recently asked her class 'What are clouds made of?' The responses were many and varied. Some thought they were made of smoke, some had fuzzy notions about them being made over the sea, but they were unclear of the process. On the other hand, another child, the son of a local meteorologist, was able to talk about evaporation and had a clear schema of the water cycle. There was, then, tremendous variation in the schemas held by the children in that class. The teacher's job there, as in any classroom, was to find effective ways of modifying, extending or elaborating the children's schemas. Indeed, we can define learning in these terms as the extension, modification or elaboration of existing cognitive schemas.

That children have different schemas is, of course, one reason for the stress on individualisation of learning. But this should not be taken too far. Ideas or schema are often shared, and this is not surprising. Children who come from the same school catchment area will, for example, have shared experiences in their local environment as well as in their school; another powerful shared experience is that of television.

So, children have schemas which are differentially complete or correct, some of which are shared. But how do their schemas change in school? Teachers offer knowledge in the form of telling, demonstrating and explaining, and pupils work on different kinds of tasks or activities designed to allow the practice, development or generation of a wide range of knowledge and understanding. Most importantly, it is the child who makes sense of these inputs, by constructing links with their prior knowledge. It is assumed that the construction of links is an active intellectual process involving the generation, checking and restructuring of ideas in the light of those already held. Construction of meaning is a continuous process and this view of learning is often referred to as 'constructivist'.

There is little argument among theorists that learning involves the construction of knowledge through experience. Arguments occur in relation to the conditions under which such learning is optimised – should learning be individual or social? Bruner and Haste (1987) capture this argument well when contrasting children as 'social beings' and 'lone scientists'.

'A quiet revolution has taken place in developmental psychology in the last decade. It is not only that we have begun to think again of the child as a social being – one who plays and talks with others, learns through interactions with parents and teachers – but because we have come once more to appreciate that through such social life, the child acquires a framework for interpreting experience, and learning how to negotiate meaning in a manner congruent with the requirements of the culture. 'Making sense' is a social process; it is an activity that is always situated within a cultural and historical context.

'Before that, we had fallen into the habit of thinking of the child as an 'active scientist', constructing hypotheses about the world, reflecting upon experience, interacting with the physical environment and formulating increasingly complex structures of thought. But this active, constructing child had been conceived as a rather isolated being, working alone at her problem-solving. Increasingly we see now that, given an appropriate, shared social context, the child seems more competent as an intelligent social operator than she is as a 'lone scientist' coping with a world of unknowns.'

This support for the child as a social being rather than as a lone scientist constitutes an attack on Piaget's views of learning, which assume that genuine intellectual competence is a manifestation of a child's largely unassisted activities. Bruner (1986) stresses far more the importance of the social setting in learning. 'I have come increasingly to recognise that most learning in most settings is a communal activity, a sharing of the culture. It is not just that the child must make his knowledge his own, but that he must make it his own in a community of those who share his sense of belonging to a culture.' This leads him to emphasise the role of negotiating and sharing in children's classroom learning, and in this he has been influenced by the work of Vygotsky. Vygotsky (1978) assigned a much greater significance to the social environment than Piaget: 'Learning awakens a variety of internal developmental processes that are able to operate only when the child is interacting with people in his environment and in co-operation with his peers.' Social interaction is thus assigned a central role in facilitating learning. For Vygotsky, a child's potential for learning is revealed and indeed is often realised in interactions with more knowledgeable others. These 'more knowledgeable others' can be anybody – peers, siblings, the teacher, parents, grandparents, and so on.

One of Vygotsky's main contributions to our understanding of learning is his concept of the 'zone of proximal development', which refers to the gap between what an individual can do alone and unaided, and what can be achieved with the help of more knowledgeable others – 'What a child can do today in co-operation, tomorrow he will be able to do on his own' (Vygotsky, 1962). For him, the foundation of learning and development is co-operatively achieved success, and the basis of that success is language and communication. 'Children solve practical tasks with the help of their speech, as well as with their eyes and their hands' (Vygotsky, 1962). Through speech to themselves (inner speech) and others, children begin to organise their experiences into thought.

The belief that talk is central to learning is not new. In 1972 Britton wrote: 'We have seen that talk is a major instrument of learning in infancy; that the infant *learns by talking* and that *he learns to talk by talking* . . . they must practise language in the sense in which a doctor "practises" . . . and not in the sense in which a juggler "practises" a new trick before he performs it'. The Bullock Report (1975) devoted itself entirely to language, and welcomed the growth of interest in oral language, 'for we cannot emphasise too strongly our conviction of its importance in the education of the child.' It was argued that all schools ought to have, as a priority objective, a commitment to the speech needs of their pupils.

The National Association for the Teachers of English (NATE) neatly encapsulated the argument when stating that, 'One of the major functions of language that concerns teachers is its use for learning: for trying to put new ideas into words, for testing out one's thinking on other people, for fitting together new ideas with old ones and so on, which all need to be done to bring about new understanding. These functions suggest active uses of language by the pupil, as opposed to passive reception.'

The status of talk in the classroom was reinforced in the 1980s through the focus on oracy by the Assessment of Performance Unit (APU). From their survey of 11-year-olds they reported that gains in mastery of spoken language may have beneficial effects on pupils' learning capabilities. 'The experience of expressing and shaping ideas through talk as well as writing, and of collaborating to discuss problems or topics, help to develop a critical and exploratory attitude towards knowledge and concepts.' They concluded that 'Pupils' performances could be substantially improved if they were given regular opportunities in the classroom to use their speaking and listening skills over a range of purposes, in a relaxed atmosphere.' (APU, 1986)

Following this, the authors of the English National Curriculum recommended a separate language component for speaking and listening, thus demonstrating their belief in oracy. 'Our inclusion of speaking and listening as a separate profile component in our recommendations is a reflection of our conviction that these skills are of central importance to children's development.' (National Curriculum Council, 1989)

Hence, a constructivist view of learning perceives children as intellectually active learners already holding ideas or schema which they use to make sense of their everyday experiences. Learning in classrooms involves the extension, elaboration or modification of their schemas. This process is one by which learners actively make sense of the world by constructing meanings. Learning is optimised in settings where social interaction, particularly between a learner and more knowledgeable others, is encouraged, and where co-operatively achieved success is a major aim. The medium for this success is talk, which is now widely accepted as a means of promoting pupils' understandings and of evaluating their progress.

Implications for practice

That pupils bring schemas of their own to bear on any given topic, and that some of these will be shared and others idiosyncratic, has to be taken into account by teachers in their planning of classroom tasks. To take these schemas adequately into account necessitates a clear understanding of what they are, that is, it requires the teacher to take on the role of diagnostician (Bennett *et al.*, 1984). A useful metaphor for gaining access to children's conceptions is that of creating 'a window into the child's mind'. To open the curtains of that window often needs far more than a rudimentary look at a child's work. It demands a sophisticated combination of observation and careful questioning and this is likely to need a great deal of time.

Judging an appropriate level for a task or activity is clearly critical to the development of learning. In this context, the notion of the 'zone of proximal development' is again important; Vygotsky believed that optimal learning is that which involves the acquisition of cognitive skills slightly beyond the child's independent grasp. A similar concept is that of 'match' between task and child, about which Her Majesty's Inspectorate (HMI) have been much concerned over the past decade. Their definition, put crudely, is that tasks should be planned which are neither too difficult nor too easy for the child (HMI, 1978, 1983, 1985; see also, Bennett and Desforges, 1988). Despite 'match' or 'appropriateness' being differently defined by Vygotsky and HMI, their relationship to diagnosis is the same. Without adequate diagnosis of children's competences or understandings, it is unlikely that teacher judgements of appropriate tasks will be accurate.

Having made decisions about content, teachers then present tasks to pupils. In whatever mode this is done (demonstration, discussion, experiment, etc), pupils' construction of meanings will be facilitated by clear statements of purpose, and information about how the task fits into work previously done and its relation to that which will be tackled in the future.

The view that learning is optimised through talk in co-operative settings has implications for presentation, as well as for classroom management. The nature of the teacher's talk needs to be carefully considered, as does the kind of classroom setting which allows for peer tutoring and co-operative working between pupils.

The most explicit advice on this aspect of classroom practice is to be found in the NCC guidance on the English curriculum, particularly that on speaking and listening (NCC, 1989). Here the guidance prescribes classrooms where children feel sufficiently encouraged and secure to be able to express and explore their thoughts, feelings and emotions; where teachers encourage talk which is genuinely tentative and explanatory, while demonstrating that talk is a rigorous activity. Drawing clearly from constructivist ideas, the guidance argues that children should be able to make connections between what they already know and new experiences and ideas, and that the main vehicle for this will be their own talk. Teachers are also asked to reflect on their own questioning strategies. For example, in talking with children the teacher should ensure that questions are genuinely open-ended, that children have problems to solve without a subtly indicated, expected answer, and that they are encouraged to speculate, hypothesise, predict and test out ideas with each other and with the teacher. The emphasis should be on language being used, not to communicate what is known, but as an instrument of learning. 'It is time for children to think aloud, to grapple with ideas and to clarify thoughts.' The guidance argues that once children have developed new understandings they will need to reflect and exchange ideas and views with other pupils and the teacher in order to consolidate their learning. Such talk does, of course, also indicate to the teacher the state of the child's understanding; that is, it is an aid to diagnosis.

This guidance appears to be attempting to create what Edwards and Mercer (1987) describe as a framework for shared understanding with children, based on joint knowledge and action. This framework acts as a 'scaffold' 'for children's mental explanations, a cognitive climbing-frame – built by children with their Vygotskyan teacher – which structures activity more systematically than the discovery sand-pit of the Piagetian classroom. Talk between teachers and children helps build the scaffolding. Children's activity, even 'discovery', in the absence of such a communicative framework may, in cognitive terms, lead nowhere.'

Current practice

Having considered current perspectives on how children learn, and the implications of these perspectives for classroom practice, the critical question now to be considered is 'how does current teaching measure up?' The aim here is not to provide a complete description of present-day primary practice and analyse its strengths and weaknesses – that would need a book in itself. Rather, we will concentrate on those aspects of teaching identified in the last section: eliciting and diagnosing children's conceptions, provision and presentation of appropriate learning activities, co-operation and grouping, and the nature of classroom talk.

The use of a simple diagram of a teaching cycle allows these aspects, and their inter-relationships, to be examined. In Figure 1.1, the cycle begins with the teacher planning and preparing tasks and activities for children which are then presented in some way (eg, through discussion, an experiment, a television programme, etc). The children then engage with their work within a classroom management system set up by the teacher (eg, individuals working on individual tasks; mixed ability groups in an integrated day arrangement; the whole class working in small co-operative groups on the same technology task, etc). Once this work has been completed, it would be expected that teachers would assess or diagnose it, using that information to feed back to pupils, and to feed forward to inform their next round of planning.

Elements of this cycle are now considered in the light of recent research in classrooms.

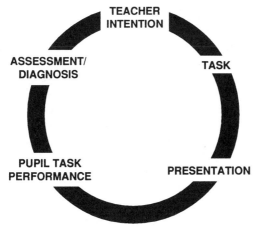

Figure 1.1 A simple teaching cycle

Planning

Typically, teachers plan around the content they intend to teach. This is clearly seen in topic-based approaches where part of a term's work will be based around a project such as 'The Victorians', 'Water' or 'Mini-beasts'. This is sensible at one level, but leads to problems at another. For example, criticism of project work by researchers (Eggleston and Kerry, 1987; HMI, 1989) centres on the dual issues of teachers being unclear about what it is they wish their pupils to learn, and an associated lack of assessment. The National Curriculum could help to some extent since teacher intentions (via statements of attainment) will be more explicit; for example, 'explain shadows as a consequence of light travelling in straight lines', 'understand scale in maps and drawings', 'enter and access information in a simple database'. We are not suggesting that teachers necessarily plan on the basis of individual statements of attainment, simply that such statements make clear what the intended learning outcome is. This in turn alerts the teacher to what ought to be assessed. In short, planning by content, as is common practice, is not always conducive to clarity about, or adequate assessment of, children's learning.

Presentation

The tasks and activities, when planned, are presented to an individual child, a group or the whole class. This presentation could simply take the form of a general direction to 'get on from where you left off yesterday', as occurs in many mathematics lessons across the nation (Bennett *et al.*, 1984), or it could be a question-and-answer session prior to a class written task, or a television programme, a science experiment and so on. Whatever mode of working is decided upon, it is critical that children are clear of the requirements, and have the necessary information and any relevant materials.

It is becoming increasingly clear how crucial presentation is in terms of children's learning. Our recent studies have highlighted how inadequately teachers of children of any age, indicate the *purpose* of activities. They are very good at telling children *what* to do, but not at telling them *why* they are doing it. This is important, since the manner in which the task is specified confers importance to certain aspects of it and ignores others. For example, in our recent study of four-year-olds in infant classes (Bennett and Kell, 1989), one teacher intended that pupils should attempt some picture sequencing – to help the children to think logically and to give them the idea of direction. The activity chosen to fulfil this intention was appropriate, comprising three pictures to be put into temporal sequence. However, it was presented with the words 'now we are going to do some colouring and cutting'. In another class, the teacher's intention was that children should practise the numbers 1–5. She planned to use a large farm layout which had different numbers of animals in the fields and farmyard. However, she presented the activity by saying 'would you like to play with the farm animals?' Observing and talking to the children after these activities made it clear that they did what the teacher had asked them to do, that is, colouring and playing with the animals; no picture sequencing or counting had taken place. The teacher's presentation had dictated the children's activity, thereby subverting their own good intentions.

Presentation is also linked to assessment. This is most clearly seen in writing activities. We have often observed in creative writing sessions that teachers called for a really exciting story with lots of imagination but actually assessed the work in terms of length, neatness and grammar. The children were alert to this. When we asked them what the teacher wanted when she asked for a really exciting story, they answered 'half a page of neat writing with full stops and capital letters'. These young children were being very clever human beings. They had recognised that what the teacher demanded was not what she assessed and rewarded, so they went for what she assessed. Whether we like it or not, children's perceptions of what is to be assessed and rewarded is what often drives classroom work. Presentation thus dictates and sometimes confuses task demand, with inevitable consequences for the quality of work produced and with important consequences for teachers' task management.

Edwards and Mercer (1987) also noted that teachers rarely informed children of purposes, but they went on to argue that this was a deliberate move on the teacher's part.

'It appears to be a valued and common practice that teachers will conduct an entire lesson, or series of lessons, and never feel it appropriate to tell the pupils why they are doing particular activities, or where it all fits into what they have done and will do next. This appears to be no accidental state of affairs. The avoidance of explicit communication of the goals and contexts of classroom activity is a consequence of teachers' educational ideology – that pupils are essentially individuals in pursuit of a realisation of their own individual potentials, that they are not to be told things, that they should learn things for themselves.'

Matching

Aligned with planning and presentation is the question of the match between task and child; that is, the extent to which the presented tasks are adequately related to children's capabilities. The Plowden Report (1967) saw this as a problem of avoiding 'The twin pitfalls of demanding too much and expecting too little', whereas a Vygotskyan view would be that we should perhaps demand a little too much, particularly in co-operative settings. Whichever view is taken, matching is a good deal easier to talk about than to achieve.

Her Majesty's Inspectorate have expressed concern at poor levels of matching ever since the Primary Survey of 1978, particularly in areas like science and topic work. Their comments in the 9–13 Middle School Survey (1983) and the 8–12 Middle School Survey (1985) are typical. In the former, they argued that 'Both the more able and less able were not given enough suitable activities in a majority of schools', and in the latter report they stated: 'Overall, the content, level of demand and pace of work were most often directed toward the children of average ability in the class. In many classes there was insufficient differentiation to cater for the full range of children's capabilities.'

This same message also features large in HMI surveys of probationary teachers. In their 1988 report, they stated that the needs of the more able and of the less able were largely ignored in three lessons out of ten, and commented that the provision of differentiated tasks is an aspect of work which presents considerable difficulties for newly trained teachers. These professional judgements of HMI accord with our research studies across the whole primary range over the last seven or eight years. In a study of top infants and bottom juniors, for example, we found a clear trend for the over-estimation of low attainers (the bottom third of children in a class) and the under-estimation of high attainers (the top third). This trend becomes even more marked if children at the extremes of ability in the class are considered (Bennett *et al.*, 1984, 1987).

Implementation

The implementation stage of the teaching cycle brings us to two important aspects of classroom practice, the management of children and the management of talk.

In considering the management of children for learning, the Plowden Report, although avowedly supporting, and indeed prescribing, individualisation, recognised a practical difficulty. If all teaching were on an individual basis, only seven or eight minutes a day would be available for each child. The report therefore advised teachers to economise by 'teaching together a small group of children who are roughly at the same stage.' Further, these groups should change in accordance with children's needs, the implication being that the class would be organised flexibly, with groups forming and re-forming according to needs and activities. Various advantages were perceived for groupwork. It would help children learn to get along together in a context where peers could help one another and realise their own strengths and weaknesses as well as those of others. It could make their meaning clearer to themselves by having to explain something to others, and children could gain some opportunity to teach as well as to learn. It was hoped that apathetic children would be infected by the enthusiasm of a group, while able children would benefit by being caught up in the thrust and counter-thrust of conversation in a small group of children similar to themselves.

Unfortunately, research on classroom grouping practices provides little support for this rosy picture. In arguing that children in the group should be 'roughly at the same stage', the Plowden Report was, in modern parlance, calling for ability grouping – and that is what tends to happen. Her Majesty's Inspectorate (1978) reported that some three-quarters of classes were grouped according to ability for maths, and that for reading, two-thirds of seven-year-olds and over one-half of nine-year-olds were grouped this way. In our national survey of open-plan schools we found a similar picture.' 60 per cent of teachers of six-year-olds and 40 per cent of teachers of ten-year-olds reported using ability groups (Bennett *et al.*, 1980).

When the focus has been narrowed to observe what actually happens in groups, some sobering findings have been reported. Boydell (1975), for example, found in her sample of informal junior classes that most of the talk was between members of the same sex, even in mixed-sex groups; that only half of the talk was concerned with their work, and that conversations tended to be short. She was therefore highly sceptical of how such patterns of interaction could fulfil the advantages perceived by Plowden. Indeed, she concluded that seating children in groups 'is no guarantee that they will talk freely about anything, let alone their work.' Almost identical findings were reported by a larger study of junior children (Galton *et al.*, 1980). Briefly, it was found that while most children sat in groups, for the great majority of the time they worked as individuals on their own tasks. While in the group, pupils spent on average two-thirds of their time interacting with no-one. Only about one-sixth of the time did they talk to another child, but most of this talk was not about their work. In this study, it was exceptional to find a group working on a co-operative group task, that is, requiring a group outcome. In other words pupils worked *in* groups, but not *as* groups.

In our own study of infant classrooms we failed to find the sex bias in talk so often found in junior classrooms, which indicates that there may be an age effect operating (Bennett *et al.*, 1984). We also found task-related talk to be considerably higher, but when this talk was analysed in more detail it showed that it was mostly of a low order; there was little explanation or knowledge sharing occurring. In language work, for example, most of the requests were for spellings. We concluded that although much of the talk was task-related, little of it was task-enhancing; that is, aiding the children to understand their work.

So what is it about typical grouping practice that produces such a dismal picture? A major weakness is that although children sit in groups there is usually no specific demand for them to work together, and rarely is a group given the opportunity to work on a group task. Our studies have shown this as clearly as Galton *et al.* (1980), who concluded, 'While in most classrooms the pupils are organised in one or more seated groups for the various activities undertaken, with few exceptions they then work largely alone, as individuals. The setting is socialised in this sense but the work is individualised.' The dearth of co-operative endeavour is also reported by HMI. Their survey of middle schools showed 'Not many opportunities are provided for extended discussion; for collaborative work in groups, or for the exercise of choice, responsibility and initiative within the curriculum' (HMI, 1983). Finally, and most recently, Tizard *et al.* (1988), from their research in infant classrooms, report that: 'Group work, where children worked cooperatively on a task or activity, for example to solve a problem or produce a joint product, occurred rarely.'

It would seem clear that the nature and quality of pupil talk leaves room for much improvement. But what of teacher–pupil interaction? Three studies allow us to gain a reasonable sense of the trends here. Galton *et al.* (1980) observed junior teachers, and remarked on the striking asymmetry of teacher–pupil interaction. 'While the "typical" teacher spends most of the lesson time interacting with pupils . . . each *individual* pupil, by contrast, interacts with the teacher for only a small proportion of his time. And most of that interaction is experienced by the pupil when the teacher is addressing the whole class.' In fact, the teacher only interacted with a child on an individual basis for an average of just over 2 per cent of the time. A similar pattern was found by Tizard *et al.* (1988) during their observations of infant classes. Teacher contact mostly took the form of individual children either listening to the teacher address the whole class or another individual child; pupils therefore had an almost entirely passive role. They concluded: 'From the child's point of view, though individual *work* is common in the infant school, individual *teaching* is not.'

They also recorded the type of teacher-to-pupil talk. Nearly 80 per cent was directly concerned with communicating facts, ideas or concepts whether by explaining, informing, demonstrating, questioning or suggesting. Clearly, then, the authors argue, 'Infant classrooms are businesslike places where much of the contact between teachers and children is concerned with the tasks in hand.' They recorded little social or personal contact, little praise (1 per cent) and very little disapproval or criticism.

The latest study to report teacher–pupil contacts in a range of primary schools classified the talk into five categories of interaction – work, monitoring, routine, disciplinary and other (PRINDEP, 1990). 'Well over a third of all interactions were about the content of the tasks which had been set, and a further fifth were concerned with checking, marking or otherwise monitoring progress. Routine matters accounted for just over a quarter, and discipline and control for one in ten.'

The same asymmetry of classroom interaction was found here as in earlier studies. Teachers may be talking for almost the whole of the teaching session but the children averaged just five work-related interactions per hour, with some having as few as two, and none having more than 11.

The PRINDEP study also carried a qualitative analysis of teacher–pupil talk, arguing, as did Edwards and Mercer (1987), that 'it is essentially in the discourse between teacher and pupils that education is done, or fails to be done.' The main points to arise out of this analysis are, briefly:

(a) Teachers ask a great many questions, reflecting, the authors argue, 'the taboo of didacticism'; that is, the belief, handed down from Plowden, that children should find things out for themselves rather than being told. Thus the teacher's task is to ask the kind of questions which would prompt them to do so. However, when examined closely, there were few questions which encouraged children to work through an idea or a problem or to build on previous learning. Many were rhetorical or pseudo-questions. Others were closed, requiring simple one-

or two-word responses, and yet others were inappropriately pitched. 'Although questions were indeed prevalent, it was nearly always the teacher who asked them.'

(b)   Generating questions with demands which match children's differing abilities is virtually impossible. Genuine dialogue with the whole class did not, therefore, occur despite the fact that some teachers attempted to maintain that illusion. The most common expedient was to pitch genuine questions at a very low level, and accept pupil responses which were barely adequate or relevant.

(c)   Hiding the differential power between teacher and taught, and giving the impression of an open and reciprocal relationship, was manifested in three ways: instructions disguised as questions, imposition disguised as choice and lavish use of praise, with the suggestion that praise can be used too often, or become a mere mannerism, and thus become devalued.

(d)   There is a reluctance to pronounce any child's response as wrong. The other factor which often determined the teacher's treatment of pupil response was its relation to the teacher's train of thought, and the extent to which it enabled her to say what she wanted to say, irrespective of its correctness or relevance.

The report concluded that the fostering of children's capabilities to talk and listen emerged as a particular issue, and supported the view of HMI that 'Where the work is less effective than it should be, it is the development of oracy that is often impoverished and given too little time . . .' (HMI, 1990).

Diagnosis

In turning now from the nature of interactions to the nature of assessment and diagnosis, there is a concern, related to the above, that if the teacher's questioning style as characterised in the PRINDEP Report is fairly typical, and if, as is reported in all three studies considered above, the individual child interacts with the teacher for a very small proportion of their time, then how can effective diagnosis be occurring? The short answer is that it probably isn't.

We referred earlier to the metaphor of 'a window into the child's mind' and argued that to see through this window needs more than a rudimentary look at a child's work. It needs a sophisticated combination of observation, questioning and listening. Thus the need for more time. What, in fact, we often find in contemporary classrooms is a great deal of assessment, often informal and unrecorded, and much assessment characterised by ticks, crosses and brief comments. There is a lack of diagnosis, and this is often accompanied by teachers concentrating on what children produce, for example, a page of completed sums, rather than on how it has been achieved. Yet both are necessary for diagnosis. An analysis of common errors in written work, or in number work, gives teachers a first glimpse through the 'window'; further questioning of the child concerning strategies used when coming to those typical errors opens the 'curtains' even wider (Bennett *et al.*, 1984; Bennett and Cass, 1989; Bennett and Kell, 1989).

Poor diagnosis has serious implications. No teacher can decide on the next optimal step for a child or children without a clear view of where they are now. It is not possible to extend or modify schemas without knowledge of those schemas. Lack of diagnosis also has substantial implications for the quality of matching and differentiation. We have argued previously that at the root of poor matching is inadequate diagnosis (Bennett *et al.*, 1984), and this is supported by HMI (1980). 'Generally, schools that had good procedures for the assessment of individual children's needs, abilities and attainments were, not surprisingly, markedly more successful in providing appropriate work for their pupils than were those schools without such procedures.'

We have also argued, on the basis of our observations in classrooms, that diagnosis cannot routinely be carried out in classrooms, even where teachers have been provided with the relevant skills, until more efficient forms of classroom management are set in place. Too often, classrooms are characterised by a management system built around the teacher attempting to be the provider of instant solutions to a constant stream of problems. This has been shown to be an inefficient and wasteful system since it devours teacher time, thus denying opportunities for monitoring and observation (Bennett *et al.*, 1984).

Summary

So how does present primary practice measure up against those features suggested as necessary for quality pupil learning? It was argued that for optimal learning the teacher has to be a good diagnostician. What we find in reality is that diagnosis rarely occurs in any structured way. Teachers are not provided with the necessary skills in their training, they tend to set up management systems which frustrate such attempts, and the type of questions they tend to ask are not effective at eliciting children's understanding. A knock-on effect of poor diagnosis is the provision of inappropriate work to children, work which is often too hard for lower attainers and too easy for high attainers.

It was argued that conditions for learning are enhanced by good presentation strategies, including informing children of the purpose of the work being done, how it fits into what has already been done, and what will be done in the future. Regrettably, however, the research indicates that this rarely happens. Teachers are generally good at telling children what to do, but not at why they are doing it.

A cornerstone of the Vygotskyan perspective is the stress on opportunities for collaboration and on the quality of interaction, but there is much room for improvement in both in British primary classrooms. According to the research undertaken, groups are rarely set up for the purpose of co-operation; indeed it is unclear for what purpose they are set up. Children sit *in* groups but do not work *as* a group. They sit together engaged on their own individual tasks and rarely interact to good effect. Neither, it would seem, do they interact with their teacher very often, except vicariously as the teacher talks to the whole class, or to the group they are sitting in. Conditions for effective learning necessitate the opportunity to express their thoughts and engage with the teacher in genuine dialogue. But classroom talk is dominated by the teacher, and, if the research is to be believed, genuine dialogue is rare.

The role of ideology

So why is practice so far out of step with current conceptions of learning? Edwards and Mercer (1987) are in no doubt, putting the blame fairly and squarely on the educational ideology advocated by the Plowden Report. 'They [teachers] have good reason for relying upon it, because it is an educational approach based on sensible criticisms of traditional, didactic teaching methods, advocated by a high status committee of educationists and legitimised by the most widely accepted theory of cognitive development.' However, along with other critics they believe that the time is ripe for a re-appraisal of this dominant ideology. 'This is largely because the Piagetian theory upon which it stands has not withstood recent critical attacks; it no longer justifies educationists' trust. It encourages a pedagogy which over-emphasises the individual at the expense of the social, which under-values talk as a tool for discovery, and which discourages teachers from making explicit to children the purposes of educational activities and the criteria for success.'

Edwards and Mercer are here reflecting the worries of educationists over the last decade or more (Galton *et al.*, 1980; Southgate *et al.*, 1981; Bennett *et al.*, 1984; HMI, 1978, 1982, 1983, 1985). Most recently, we have argued that 'the problems of matching, monitoring and diagnosis are thus intertwined, and all occur as a consequence of teachers' persistence in attempts to implement and maintain a philosophy of individualisation. It is this which is the core of the problem. And the reason is simple. Individualisation is impossible.' (Bennett and Kell, 1989). Galton *et al.* (1980) argued similarly '. . . the Plowden prescripts stressing discovery learning and the probing, questioning character of the teacher's role appear, at least with present class sizes, impossible of achievement.' Southgate *et al.* (1981) and, more recently, Topping (1988), were both concerned by individualisation in the context of reading. Topping commented:

> 'For one teacher with a class of 30 pupils to serve as an efficient and effective direct educator is frankly impossible, as any teacher who has desperately tried to hear every member of a primary school class reading every day will readily agree. All too often this ends up with one child reading to the teacher, while another dozen wait at the teacher's desk for attention in respect of other problems; administrative interruptions and problems with deviant behaviour compound the awfulness of the situation. Omniscience is not a contractual requirement. Teachers must increasingly function as managers of effective learning, rather than the font of all available wisdom.'

The message is clear. Individualisation, based on the notion of the child as a 'lone scientist', needs balancing with a pedagogy which allows the child to take on the role of a 'social being', in a move from individualistic to co-operative classroom endeavours.

2   Co-operative grouping

Rationale

In Chapter 1, we saw that current views on children's learning stress the use of language through co-operative endeavours. But there are other powerful reasons for considering the implementation of co-operation in classrooms, some directly relevant to the National Curriculum. In the English curriculum, for example, the attainment targets for speaking and listening include one which specifically demands the assessment of co-operation. To meet this target children should be able, along with other skills, to:

Level 1   Speak freely, and listen, one-to-one to a peer.

Level 2   Present real or imaginary events in a connected narrative to a small group of peers.

Level 3   In a range of activities (including problem-solving), speak freely, and listen, to a small group of peers.

Level 4   Describe an event or experience to a group of peers, clearly and audibly and in detail. Give and receive precise instructions and follow them. Ask relevant questions with increasing confidence. Offer a reasoned explanation of how a task has been done or a problem has been solved. Take part effectively in a small-group discussion and respond to others in the group.

Level 5   Speak freely and audibly to a large audience of peers and adults. Discuss and debate constructively, advocating and justifying a particular point of view. Contribute effectively to a small-group discussion which aims to reach agreement on a given assignment.

The importance of this particular attainment target is its cross-curricular role. Although included in the English curriculum it can be met through any curriculum context.

A second aspect bearing directly on the successful implementation of the National Curriculum is making time to assess children's progress continuously. This is an area of considerable concern to teachers. The following typical comment, from a teacher in a national survey we carried out on the implementation of the National Curriculum, exemplifies this.

'In principle it would appear that the national curriculum has a lot to offer. However, with the extra demands of record keeping, testing and marking, it makes me wonder if we will have time enough to teach.'

When we asked which 'professional skills' teachers found hardest to implement in the classroom, seven in every ten identified the diagnosis of children's learning difficulties; nearly two-thirds cited continuous assessment of children's work and nearly one-half said record keeping (Wragg, Bennett and Carré, 1989).

Teachers' anxieties in these areas are easy to understand. It is becoming increasingly clear how important assessment is in relation to both teacher planning and pupil learning. As the Task Group on Assessment (TGAT, 1988) argued,

'Assessment should be an integral part of the education process, continually providing both "feedback" and "feedforward". It therefore needs to be incorporated systematically into teaching strategies and practices.'

However as we suggested in Chapter 1, the kind of diagnostic assessment necessary to uncover pupils' conceptions takes time. Marking a page of sums can be relatively speedy; probing a child's understanding of 'equivalence' or 'scale' takes considerably longer. So the question naturally arises – where is this time to come from?

Classroom time is a scarce resource, and teachers need to learn how to manage it more effectively (Bennett, 1987). As Lemlech (1988) has argued, 'A good organisation creates time', but as we have already seen, teachers often allow themselves to be bombarded with pupil demands that eat up their time. Let us consider an actual example of this kind of problem.

Matthew is working by himself on a series of maths tasks in a classroom where the majority of children seem interested in their work, they are concerned with 'getting on' as fast as they can and they are well-acquainted with the classroom routines and the teacher's expectations. Although there are occasional arguments, particularly over necessary materials such as rubbers, the children are supportive and friendly towards the members of their group, helping when asked, voluntarily offering assistance, and organising each other.

However, Matthew, an able seven-year-old, makes persistent demands on his teacher. (The following description is not a summary of all Matthew's activities, but shows the times of demands on the teacher in one lesson, as well as some explanation for them.) Remember, too, that Matthew is just one in a class of thirty.

9.37   Matthew starts work on the first problem immediately, then stops to chat and look around the room. When the teacher approaches, he asks, 'Mrs Stevenson, do you write the question?' The teacher replies, 'Yes, if it's the sort you write the question. Do you think you write the question?'

9.45   Matthew goes to the teacher to ask about the layout of the third question and he is told to 'Just do them underneath, like that.' He returns to his place, rapidly completes the multiplication tables and within two minutes has returned to the teacher, again asking about the layout. His work is marked and he goes back to his seat . . .

9.48   However, as soon as he has read the next question on his card, he gets up again, goes to the teacher . . .

9.57   He goes to ask the teacher where the weights are and is told, 'Oh, Miss Bradley's got them. Go and say, "Please Miss Bradley can we have our grams back?" . . .' (He does so.)

10.06   Matthew goes up to the teacher's desk and waits for a few minutes. He says, 'Mrs Stevenson, I've done the next column,' and she asks him a series of questions about the work he has just completed.

10.21   Matthew goes to the teacher's table.
    Teacher   'What does it say?'
        (He has written the wrong answer)
    Teacher   'Well, why have you put $\frac{1}{2}$ to 3? This writing's very poor. Come on, tell me what it says.'

He reads out the correct answer and is told to go and make his work a bit neater.

10.23 He rubs out some work and writes it neatly. Matthew goes back to the teacher.

Teachers will recognise this child's behaviour as fairly typical and, when multiplied by the number of children in the class, can judge how much of their time is taken up with this kind of demand.

Briefly stated, then,

(a)   there are enormous demands made on teachers' time in the classroom;

(b)   this time could be better managed;

(c)   there is an urgent need to create more time to improve monitoring and diagnosis.

There would seem to be several ways of helping to create the required time. Some would require political and economic will, such as the provision of non-contact time for primary teachers, which is long overdue, a further decrease of class sizes, or the implementation of a continental type of day. However, these structural changes seem unlikely in the near, or even distant, future, and so attention needs to be paid to changes at the school and/or classroom level.

At the school level there has been much progress in involving parents in the education of their children both within and outside the school. To create time, parents need to work inside the school, indeed inside the classroom, to substitute for the teacher in some of the more mundane, less skilful aspects of teaching. This has proved to be a valuable innovation particularly where there has been some in-school training for the parents so that their role and function in the classroom are clear and their interactions with teachers purposeful. Unfortunately, the converse can apply – poor training and lack of clarity about roles can actually increase teachers' management problems.

We feel that parental partnership of this kind has great potential and should continue, but that a more permanent solution lies in the teacher embracing alternative, more efficient, organisation and management styles. We thus decided in our recent work with teachers to record informally the nature and frequency of the pupil requests made of them. The vast majority were low-level demands. The range was wide, covering requests relating to task management; for example, dates, use of margins, in 'rough' or 'best', materials, in-flight checks on their work, complaints about other pupils behaviour, routine; and so on (Dunne and Bennett, 1990). Few required the pedagogic skills of a trained teacher, but in combination they blocked the teachers using their skills to better ends. What is clearly required, therefore, is a system which clears the teacher of this responsibility, thereby creating time. An effective system, we hypothesised, would be created by making the co-operative group the source of reference for its members, rather than the teacher. The extent to which this hypothesis was supported will be presented in Chapter 3.

The final reason for co-operation in the classroom considered here is the wider societal one. Schmuck (1985) makes the broad point in the following extract.

'Why have we humans been so successful as a species? We are not strong like tigers, big like elephants, protectively coloured like lizards, or swift like gazelles. We are intelligent, but an intelligent human alone in the forest would not survive for long. What has really made us such successful animals is our ability to apply our intelligence to co-operating with others to accomplish group goals. From the primitive hunting group to the corporate boardroom, it is those of us who can solve problems while working with others who succeed. In fact, in modern society, co-operation in face-to-face groups is increasingly important. A successful scientist must be able to co-operate effectively with other scientists, with technicians, and with students. An executive must co-operate with other executives, salespersons, suppliers, and superiors. Of course, each of those relationships also has competitive elements, but in all of them, if the participants cannot co-operate to achieve a common goal, all lose out. It is difficult to think of very many adult activities in which the ability to co-operate with others is not important. Human society is composed of overlapping co-operating groups: families, neighbourhoods, work groups, political parties, clubs, teams.

Because schools socialise children to assume adult roles, and because co-operation is so much a part of adult life, one might expect that co-operative activity would be emphasised. However, this is far from true. Among the prominent institutions of our society, the schools are least characterised by co-operative activity.'

Schmuck is commenting on the situation in North America, but it is similar in Britain. Schmuck's point about schools failing to prepare for, or link into, the nation's economic needs is echoed in the British context by Salter and Tapper (1981). They argue that schools place a high value on knowledge that is of only marginal relevance to the economy. Further, '. . . we have a work force that no longer has the technical competence to compete in the international market and we have forms of social control (in schools) that make it difficult to rectify this state of affairs.'

Cowie and Rudduck (1988) argue that groupwork in industry is valued in two main ways; first, as a means of forging and sustaining interpersonal relations (eg, building morale, team spirit, solving interpersonal problems, managing work groups, etc); and second, as an effective means of solving work-related problems (eg, generating ideas, increasing productivity, pooling areas of expertise, and communicating ideas). There is no doubt that there is an increasing call for young people, whether straight from school or from higher education, to have the capacity to work co-operatively with others. 'The great majority of learners are destined for a productive life of practical action. They are going to do things in most part in cooperation with other people.' (Royal Society of Arts, 1983).

Co-operative learning can thus be justified in terms of children's learning, the effective implementation of the National Curriculum and society's economic future. Notwithstanding this we ought to make it quite clear, before considering such grouping in the classroom, that we are not advocating a wholesale shift to groupwork. What we contend is that a better balance needs to be achieved between individual, group and whole-class work. With that important proviso let us now consider what co-operative grouping actually looks like.

Co-operative groups

Co-operative groups in reality look little different from those which teachers currently set up. The crucial differences are in the nature of the tasks set and the demands for co-operation that they contain. The groups most used by teachers are of two types, as shown below.

Figure 2.1 represents four children (*) as a group sitting together, but working on their own individual tasks (a, b, c, d) and aiming for an individual outcome or product.

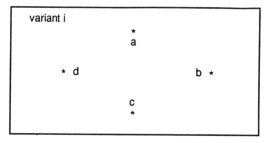

Figure 2.1 Children working individually on individual tasks for individual products

This arrangement is widespread, and seen typically in maths where children often work on the same structured scheme, but at different stages within it. This occurs whether or not children are grouped by ability.

The second variant shown in Figure 2.2 is more common in writing where teachers will often set a class task, to be completed individually (eg the writing of a story). Here the children (*) are engaged on the same task (a) but again the aim is for an individual, not a group, outcome – each has to write their own story.

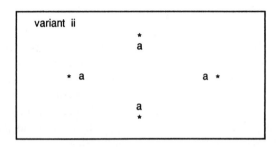

Figure 2.2 Children working individually on identical tasks for individual products

The demand for co-operation is apparent in neither type of group, although it would be easier to achieve in the set-up of Figure 2.2. Indeed, children often seem confused in this situation about whether they are allowed to co-operate or not. The point to bear in mind, however, is that it is these types of group that tend to generate talk of low quality, often not related to the tasks being worked on. What seems to have happened in practice is that teachers have taken on board the views of the Plowden Report (1967) on having children work in groups, but have preferred to retain individualisation rather than co-operation in that context. As Alexander (1984) wrote:

> 'Grouping thus emerges as an organisational device rather than as a means of promoting more effective learning, or perhaps exists for no reason other than that fashion and ideology dictate it.'

There is, on the other hand, a wide variety of types of co-operative groups, all American, with a bewildering array of names – STAD, Jigsaw, Coop-Coop, etc (*cf* Kagan, 1985). In our work with teachers we have tended to use two versions, modified to fit the British primary classroom, together with a third type which is a simple modification of the variant in Figure 2.2. These are described below.

What characterises each group is a demand for co-operation, but the nature of that demand is somewhat different in each case. Variant (iii) (Figure 2.3) is in fact (ii) (Figure 2.2) with a teacher demand for co-operation. When children are working on the same task it is possible for them to share the experience and contribute to each other's interest, motivation or understanding. Their talk may influence each other's actions, ideas and the quality of the end product. But it is unlikely that this will occur unless the teacher specifically demands and encourages this kind of behaviour. However, since children are asked for individual products, the task does not in itself demand co-operation.

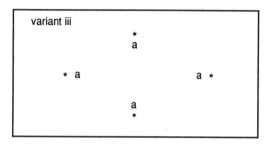

Figure 2.3 Children working individually on identical tasks for individual products

Variant (iv) (Figure 2.4) is the first of the truly co-operative group types. It is a modification of that developed by Aronson (1978). In this kind of group, the task is divided into as many parts as there are group members – in this case, four (a1, a2, a3, a4). Each child works on one part of the task, the task being divided in such a way that the group outcome cannot be achieved until every group member has successfully completed their piece of work. At this point the 'jigsaw' can be fitted together. Co-operation is thus built into the task structure, as indeed is individual accountability. It is difficult in this type of group task for a child to sit back and let others do all the work, especially since group members are likely to ensure that everyone pulls their weight. Examples of such tasks would be the production of a group story or newspaper, or the making of a 'set' of objects in a practical maths activity.

For the type of task in Figure 2.5, adapted from Johnson and Johnson (1975), children will need to work co-operatively since only one product will be required of the group. Activities will therefore have to be co-ordinated and it is possible that a group leader will emerge in order to create the necessary organisation. Each individual's work will

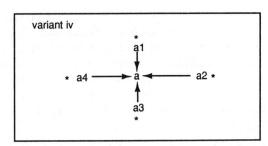

Figure 2.4 Children working individually on 'Jigsaw' elements for a joint outcome

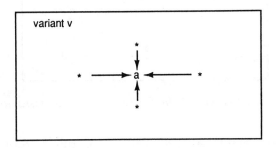

Figure 2.5 Children working jointly on one task for a joint outcome (or discussion)

have an impact on the group product but will be worthless until it becomes part of that product. Examples can be seen in problem-solving in technology, construction activities or in discussion tasks.

Although collaborative endeavour is necessary for the group to succeed, it is less easy to ascertain exactly what each pupil has contributed and individual accountability is therefore lower.

These three models demonstrate that co-operative groupwork is not a single, specific form of classroom organisation but encompasses different approaches, different types of task and different demands for co-operation.

The two co-operative models (Figures 2.4, 2.5) have had to be adapted from American sources because in our view teachers would find the original forms less acceptable. To illustrate this, the original form of Jigsaw is briefly outlined below (Kagan, 1985).

The original Jigsaw method was developed to place students in situations of extreme interdependence. Each student is provided with only part of the materials of an academic unit but is evaluated on how well he or she masters the whole unit. In a sense, each student on a learning team has but one piece of a jigsaw puzzle; the learning task for each student is to obtain the information from every piece of the puzzle. To do well, the students have to learn the unique information possessed by every other member (see Aronson, 1978). The elements of the original Jigsaw method include the following:

Specifically designed curriculum materials

The curriculum materials are designed or rewritten so that each member of a learning team has a unique source that is comprehensible without reference to other sources.

Team-building and communication training

Because communication among team members is an essential part of Jigsaw, special team-building and communication training activities are included to prepare students to co-operate and communicate in groups. Team-building is extensive; it involves role-playing, brainstorming, and specially designed group activities.

Student group leader

During the extensive team-building, the importance of a group leader is stressed. Group leaders are selected by the teacher, and they receive special training, including discussions and role-playing. The group leader is expected to help organise the group, to keep the group on task, to serve as the group–teacher liaison, to model productive social and academic behaviours, and to help resolve conflicts.

Teams

Teams range in size from three to seven members but five- or six-member teams are recommended. The students are assigned to teams so that the teams will be heterogeneous with regard to ability level, race and sex, and personality factors such assertiveness. The teachers are to use their knowledge and intuition in forming groups.

Expert groups

Each team member is assigned to an expert group composed of the members of other teams who have been assigned the same expert topic. The students meet in expert groups to exchange information and to master the material each student is to present to his or her team.

Individual assessment and reward

The students take individual tests or quizzes covering all of the material of the learning unit; there is no group reward.

The original version required specially designed materials, demanded extensive training, the teacher selected a group leader, and the group always had to be mixed ability. Pupils first studied in 'expert' groups to learn their part of the task before returning to their 'own' group, all pupils were tested and given individual, not group, rewards – in all, a package not likely to win the favour of British primary teachers.

Nevertheless, this example serves to raise several pertinent issues to which we will return at various points in this book. These include the design of group tasks, group composition, training of pupils in groupwork skills, and methods of group assessment.

Research on co-operative groups

We have presented a theoretical justification for groupwork, but what evidence is there that it works in practice? One difficulty in answering this question is that virtually all research on co-operative groups has been carried out in North America. There, the use of classroom groups of any description is rare, and much of the research effort has been in the evaluation of the implementation of experimental grouping models of a highly prescriptive nature. What is more, the same person has often been the developer of the group models, the evaluator and the reviewer of the research. As we have argued elsewhere (Bennett, 1985), caution is needed in the interpretation of these reviews, 'since the conclusions reached occasionally appear to reflect the reviewers' own predilections as much as the findings themselves.'

Two sets of studies are relevant to the question of group effectiveness. The first have, as indicated above, implemented a particular group model, and tested children at the beginning and end of the implementation to assess change. Change has sometimes been in relation to gains in achievement or in some form of social development. These studies are designed to ascertain *that* groups work, not *how* they work. For this reason, we label these 'Product studies'. A separate set of studies have considered how groups work, investigating social interaction patterns and their relationships to achievement or social outcomes. We call these 'Process studies'.

Product studies

The claims made by this group of studies are impressive, and for the purposes of this exposition a selection of conclusions from the three most prolific reviewers are presented below under the sub-headings of achievement and social development.

(a) Achievement

'In our studies, we have found considerable evidence that co-operative learning experiences promote higher achievement than do competitive and individualistic learning experiences. Of the 26 studies that we have done that include achievement data, in 21 studies co-operative learning promoted higher achievement, 2 studies had mixed results, and 3 found no differences among conditions. These studies have included college studies and students from every grade but the eighth grade. They have used curriculum in maths, English, language arts, geometry, social studies, science, physical science, and physical education. The studies have lasted from one day to nine months. They have included both males and females; upper-middle-class, middle-class, working-class, and lower-class students; gifted, medium-ability, and low-ability students; and students from a number of minority groups. The length of the instructional sessions has varied from 15 to 90 minutes. The adaptability of co-operative learning is illustrated by the fact that, in these 26 studies, high, medium, and low-ability students were mixed within the co-operative learning groups. Clearly, the high-ability students did not suffer from working with medium and low-ability students. In the 4 studies that measured the achievement of gifted students separately, 3 found that they achieved higher when collaborating with medium and low-ability students, and one found no difference in achievement. In the 13 studies that measured the achievement of academically handicapped students, 12 found that they achieved higher in the co-operative condition, and one found no difference in achievement. It is evident, therefore, that co-operative learning procedures can provide appropriate instructional experiences for diverse students who work together.' (Johnson and Johnson, 1985)

'Results reported on the effects of all team-learning methods on academic achievement reflect superior performance of pupils in the small group as compared to those in the traditional classroom.' (Sharan, 1980)

'... over the past 15 years there has arisen a new interest in co-operative learning methods designed for use not as a supplement to traditional instructional methods but as a coherent alternative means of organising the classroom for instruction in fundamental curriculum areas, from mathematics to language arts to science and social studies ... Research has established that under certain circumstances the use of co-operative learning methods increases student achievement more than traditional instructional practices.' (Slavin, 1987)

(b) Social development

'In our studies, we have found considerable evidence that co-operative learning experiences promote greater interpersonal attraction and more positive relationships among students than do competitive and individual-istic learning experiences. Of the 37 studies that we have done that include interpersonal attraction data, in 35 studies co-operative learning promoted greater interpersonal attraction, and in 2 the results were mixed. These findings resulted for a wide variety of age levels, subject areas, diverse students, and instructional sessions.' (Johnson and Johnson, 1985)

'Numerous and consistently positive effects on affective and social variables have been reported in many of the co-operative team-learning studies with all methods . . . Many studies confirmed that team learning clearly increased helping behaviour, perceptions of giving and receiving help, and a sense of being able to cope with classroom studies. Furthermore, it seems reasonable to argue that the helping behaviour structured and stimulated by team learning may be related to the pervasive finding, reported often in this literature, that pupils feel more liked, more accepted, and more concerned about each other than in other forms of classroom learning. Giving and receiving help, feeling accepted by others (including the teacher), viewing situations from the perspective of others, certainly form an appropriate basis for expecting a more highly developed sense of fairness, even altruism, in sharing resources or rewards with others, which has also been found in several studies . . .

Most of the research studies which assessed race relations in the desegregated classroom as a function of interaction and peer helping in teams reported positive effects. In most cases gains in cross-racial relations were modest. Nevertheless, it seems clear that team learning, in its various manifestations, promotes positive inter-ethnic contact under co-operative conditions.' (Sharan, 1980)

'These [co-operative] methods consistently improve student self-esteem and social relations among students, in particular, race relations and acceptance of mainstreamed students.' (Slavin, 1987)

There is strong agreement by these American reviewers on core findings relating to gains in achievement, and in social and affective areas. Disputes abound in this, as in every, field. However, these are not disputes about whether co-operative groups are effective or not, but which type of group works best with what kind of task demand, in what kind of context, and with what age of children.

Finally, although they would not claim their reports to be research, it is useful to record that HMI also appear convinced of the value of co-operative groups in improving achievement. For example, in their report on mathematics in the primary school (HMI, 1989b), they wrote, 'Co-operative work was a strong and distinctive feature of the best mathematics work seen, with pupils seeking together a solution to an intellectual or practical problem.'

Process studies

What happens in groups to make them effective? How do these effects occur?

It has been argued that the investigation of the cognitive aspects of small-group learning is still in an embryonic stage (Sharan, 1980), a view shared by Webb (1982), who complained that group interaction processes have rarely been systematically investigated. Again the majority of studies are North American and it is not always clear what kind of group model is being studied. Typically the studies have been of short duration (two weeks or less), limited to maths or computing, have a group size of four children – one high ability, two average and one low – studying tasks individually within a group context.

The most common aspects of social interaction investigated in groups are various kinds of helping behaviour, and here it is necessary to distinguish between receiving help and giving it. For the receiving of help to be effective for learning there must be an explanation rather than a straight answer, it must be provided in response to a pupil's needs, and be understandable. Webb (1989) suggests that the effectiveness of help received may constitute a continuum, that is, receiving explanations is sometimes helpful, receiving information has mixed or no effect, and receiving only the answer is harmful. As Webb explains:

'A student who makes an error or asks a question about how to solve the problem clearly has a difficulty, whether a misunderstanding or lack of understanding. It seems reasonable, then, that receiving less than an explanation is not sufficient for learning. For example, it may be impossible for most students to locate their error or to figure out how to solve the problem from only the correct answer. Receiving no response at all allows even less chance to determine how to solve the problem. Similarly, a student who asks only for information would not benefit from receiving no reply. Not only would we expect these responses to have no benefit, motivational implications may account for the observed negative relationships. Receiving less help than needed may negatively

re-inforce asking for help. Receiving inadequate help may raise students'
level of frustration and, consequently, may lead them to expend less
effort on the task.'

Most studies have shown that giving explanations is positively related
to achievement, although giving low-level help is not. It also appears
that high ability children are the main sources of help in mixed ability
groups. Many teachers seem to worry, or worry that parents will
worry, about what high attainers get out of helping other children.
Webb (1989) explains this as follows:

> In explaining to someone else, the helper must clarify, organise and
> possibly re-organise the material (see Bargh and Schul, 1980). In the
> process of clarifying and re-organising the material, the helper may
> discover gaps in his or her own understanding or discrepancies with
> others' work or previous work. To resolve these discrepancies, the helper
> may search for new information and subsequently resolve those
> inconsistencies, thereby learning the material better than before.
>
> Furthermore, when an explanation given to a team-mate is not
> successful (the team-mate does not understand it or does not use it to
> solve the problem correctly), the helper is forced to try to formulate the
> explanation in new or different ways. This may include using different
> language, such as translating unusual or unfamiliar language into familiar
> language (Noddings, 1985); generating new or different examples; linking
> examples to the target student's prior knowledge or work completed
> previously; using alternative symbolic representations of the same material
> (eg, pictures vs. diagrams vs. words vs. numbers vs. symbols); and
> translating among different representations of the same material. All of
> these activities will likely expand and solidify the helper's understanding
> of the material. Giving only the answer or other low-level information,
> on the other hand, would be less likely to cause the helper to clarify or
> re-organise his or her own thinking.'

Studies on the effect of different group composition on group processes
are rare, and hence the evidence is inconclusive. As a consequence,
Bennett and Cass (1988) set up a study in Britain to contrast the effects
of three types of group – ability groups of high, average and low
attainers; mixed ability groups containing a high, an average and a
low child; and mixed groups containing only high and low attainers
– one type was composed of two high and one low pupil (2HL) and
the other, two low attainers and one high (2LH). The groups all
worked on the same task concerning co-operative decision-making on
settlement patterns, and all children were interviewed individually after
the task to establish their degree of understanding.

The findings included:

(a)   Groups 2LH performed much better than groups 2HL. In the latter combination, the low attainer seemed to be ignored, or to opt out, and as a consequence misunderstood the basis on which decisions were being made, and presented incorrect reasons in the post-task interview.

(b)   Ability groups of high attainers significantly and consistently outperformed the groups of average and low attainers. The high ability group was, overall, the best of all nine groups studied. On the other hand, the suggestion from previous research that homogeneous groups of low ability children may not have the relevant skills and knowledge to give effective explanations does gain support. Their level of instructional talk was very low, and of the 155 explanations sampled in this study only five were provided by the low ability group. The frequency of suggestions was also very low, and a proportionately large number of incorrect reasons were noted in the post-task interview. This fairly dismal picture of the processes in the low attaining group is not dissimilar to that found in the average attaining group.

(c)   High attaining children performed well, irrespective of the type of group they were in. These children talked more, and more of their talk was instructional in nature. They made the most suggestions, and had the most suggestions accepted. They provided twice as many explanations as other groups, with three-quarters of all explanations falling into the 'correct and appropriate' category. They were also the most successful at giving reasons for the decisions made in the post-task interviews. It is important to record this success of high attainers since there is a fear among many teachers that grouping such children with low attainers adversely affects the high attainer. The two major findings of this study would argue for the obverse of that.

Summary

The theoretical support for co-operative endeavours appears to be borne out by the research evidence, which shows consistent improvements in achievement, and in social and affective areas. How these improvements occur through group interaction is not totally understood, but current evidence points to the provision of appropriately timed, understandable explanations. It seems that high attainers are the major source of these explanations, and that they gain from the clarification and re-organisation of their thinking. The poor performance of average and of low ability groups has obvious implications for classroom organisation.

It is worth repeating, however, that much of this evidence is American, and that none of that research actually investigated normal classroom practice. Classrooms were simply the site in which models of group learning were implemented or tested out. All required a marked re-organisation of normal classroom practice both in grouping and in curriculum content. It is not surprising, therefore, that the process of teacher-initiated implementation and the role of the teacher in that process, has been totally ignored. Yet detail on classroom implementation is crucial. There is little point in demonstrating to teachers the theoretical and empirical utility of an approach unless the issues involved in setting it up can also be demonstrated; for example, the implications for classroom organisation, for the planning and preparation of tasks, for changes in the roles of teachers and pupils, and for assessment practices. It is to provide information on these issues that the study with teachers, reported in the next chapters, was set up.

3   Group and classroom processes

The aims of the study reflected our concerns to aid the process of implementing co-operative grouping. Some of these aims focussed on classroom processes, and the role of the teacher in implementation; others related more specifically to group processes in order to explore ill-understood issues such as the impact of type of task on group interaction. These aims are contained in the following questions:

1   Group processes

(a)   What impact do differences in task-demand have on group talk?

(b)   The three types of co-operative group used each carry a different demand for co-operation. Is this difference reflected in group talk?

2   Classroom processes

(c)   What changes do the implementation of co-operative groups have on:
- classroom management
- the teacher's role
- the quality of the children's work?

(d)   Does changing the pattern of pupil requests and demands create time for the teacher?

In seeking to answer these questions we worked with 15 primary teachers who, between them, taught the full primary age-range from 4–12 years. None of them had used co-operative grouping in their class previously. All of them had in common that they were attending a module on co-operative learning, run by the authors, either for a further degree or as an in-service course. Each agreed to modify their classroom grouping practices in order to implement one of the three variants of grouping described in the previous chapter (variants (iii) to (iv) in Figures 2.3 to 2.5 – these will now be referred to as models 1, 2 and 3, respectively). This choice was left entirely to them, as indeed was the curriculum area in which they wished to operate this system. The results of these choices are shown in Table 3.1. Most teachers opted for model 3 – working co-operatively for a group outcome – and their choices of curriculum resulted in an even split of language and maths/technology tasks.

Table 3.1 Curriculum areas and types of group

Curriculum	Model 1	Model 2	Model 3	Total
Language	4		12	16
Maths		6	1	7
Technology	1		5	6
Computers			2	2
Total	5	6	20	31

Having made these choices they then worked co-operatively in their chosen curriculum area in order to plan and design the tasks to be used with their classroom groups. The choice of activity was again left entirely to their professional judgements, although of course they had been made aware of the different requirements for a group, as opposed to an individual, task.

It was agreed that the study should take place in each class over a period of half a term, about six weeks. During that period the following data were collected.

(a) **Group processes.** The talk of each co-operative group was recorded twice, once early in the period, and the other towards the end. For this recording, each child in the group was fitted with a radio-microphone in order to gain recordings of high quality for later transcription. The length of recording varied according to the task being worked on, but ranged from between 30 and 45 minutes.

The children were usually fitted with the radio-microphones before the task was actually recorded so that they could ask questions about them and indulge themselves in what we colloquially call 'microphone talk'.

(b) Classroom processes. Most of the information on classroom processes was collected or supplied by the teachers, but these were supported by the data of a trained observer on the two days on which group recordings were being made. This information was in various forms, some systematic, some judgmental or reflective.

The most systematic data were those collected on changing the pattern of pupil requests. Prior to the actual study the teachers worked together to develop and pilot an observation schedule that they themselves could use for monitoring the pattern of requests as a normal part of their teaching. Figure 3.1 is an example of a completed schedule. The ten categories of pupil request are shown down the left-hand side of the sheet, and this particular schedule is divided up into five-minute segments covering half-an-hour's teaching. This is not strictly necessary, but was used to ascertain if patterns of requests changed through a lesson.

Brief descriptions of the meanings and examples of the categories are as follows:

1   **Instruction** – relating to lack of, or misunderstanding of, specific content or concept.

2   **Presentation** – queries relating to what has to be done in content terms ie, to task instructions.

3   **Management (a) procedure** – relating to the manner of completion of work: 'Do I need a margin?'; 'Should I draw a graph or a table?'

4   **Management (b) behaviour** – 'Please, Miss, John's kicking me'; 'The group is being silly'.

5   **Evaluation (a) interim** – requests for in-flight checks – 'Am I doing it right?'

6   **Evaluation (b) final** – end of task

7   **Transitions** – 'What should I do now?'

8   **Spellings**

9   **Materials** – 'Can I use the glue?'; 'Can I borrow a rubber?'

10   **Routine** – 'Can I go to the toilet?'

Teachers completed this schedule before they started to use co-operative groups, and again after they had done so. A check on these patterns was carried out by the observer during the two days of group recording.

Pupil demand classification		TASK:INTEGRATED DAY (27 DEMANDS)					PRE-GROUPING	
		0	5	10	15	20	25	30
1	Instruction	✓✓		✓				
2	Presentation							
3	a) Procedure Management			✓✓		✓✓	✓	
4	b) Behavior		✓	✓		✓		
5	a) interim Evaluation	✓	✓✓✓✓✓ (Maths)	✓	✓	✓		
6	b) final				✓	✓	✓✓✓ (End of maths)	
7	Transitions	✓			✓	✓	✓	
8	Spellings							
9	Materials							
10	Routine							

Figure 3.1 **Pupil request schedule**

The observations were supplemented by teacher accounts of changes in classroom organisation and management necessitated by the new grouping arrangements; reflective accounts of their own role and actions in this process; perceptions of what difficulties and/or successes arose; and their professional judgements of the quality of pupil work in the groups, and how this compared to previous work.

The findings are now considered under the two general headings of group processes and classroom processes.

Group processes

Analysis of group talk is a time-consuming business requiring several stages. The talk of each individual child is first transcribed, then all the transcriptions of individual members of the group have to be combined on the same time base. Only then can group talk begin to be categorised.

The categories used to classify group talk obviously depend on the questions being asked. We wanted a system of categories which was capable of generating conceptual links between task-demand and group talk. The conceptualisation we found most useful for this purpose was Piaget's (1959) model of the development of children's conversations. Despite this model being developed many years ago, the categories comprising the model allow both an analysis of the nature of the demand for talk, in terms of an action-abstract dimension, and of ways in which talk is managed, on an agreement-disagreement dimension. The stages that Piaget proposed for young children are shown in Figure 3.2. Briefly, Piaget argued that after children have progressed through the pre-conversational stage, various types of more developed interaction or conversation become apparent. These depend on whether the interaction is based on agreement or disagreement, and operate at different levels of collaboration in terms of action and abstract thought. It is only the conversation at stage 3 which provokes any real interchange of thought.

Our concern was not with developmental aspects of this model; we simply used it as a heuristic to derive the seven modes of group interaction shown in Table 3.2. The definitions of these modes, and examples, are presented below.

Mode A – Collective monologue   In the context of a group, but when a child's talk is to the self, without any obvious expectation of a reply; sometimes mumbling or under the breath; egocentric in nature. In the example below, the child talks to herself as she measures; other group members pay no attention.

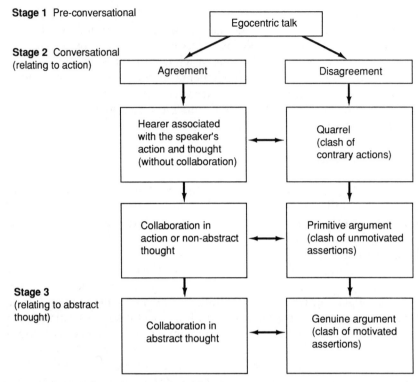

Figure 3.2 The development of childrens' conversations

Table 3.2 Conversational modes

	Stage	Conversational type	Mode
	1	Collective monologue	A
Action	2	Association with	B
		Sharing in	C
		Collaboration in	D
		Quarrelling	E
		Primitive argument	F
Abstract thought	3	Collaboration	G
		Genuine argument	H

'I need a pencil . . . I need thirty two – that's the end. Thirty three . . . thirty two . . . 1, 2, 3, 4, 5, 6 . . . 32.'

Mode B – Association with (action)   Talking about one's own activity or commenting on it; conversational and addressed to the whole group or any group member but not always specifically; not actually collaborative. This is likely to occur when the task demand is the same for all children but there is a request for individual products. For example,

'He's got tears coming down from his eyes – dripping in between his fingers.'

'Neil, look at my bog frog. Look at my frog – there – frogs by the score!'

'Oh, I like your man – it's good.'

Mode C – Sharing in (action)   Talk centres around a shared activity, often involving demonstration, and may be a response to a request for help. As for mode B, this is likely to occur when there is a request for individual products but the task demand is the same for all children. It also occurs in collaborative tasks with a single product when children interact with individuals rather than the whole group. For example,

each child in a group is making a box from a piece of squared paper. To do this, it is necessary to cut out the corners:

James: Do you just go up two by two?
Natalie: One, two. One, two. One, two. [She demonstrates how to count and where to cut out the appropriate squares from each other.]

Mode D – Collaboration in (action or non-abstract thought)   A group of children are collaborating in their activity and the talk demonstrates this. For example,

a group of children are making a cart together; most of their talk is similar to that of the discussion below:

Stacey: Come on. Let's begin.
David: Here's our instructions . . .
Stacey: Wait a minute, two centimetres on each end, make sure you add on two centimetres.
David: Make sure you add on two centimetres from each end . . . Because look . . . measure across the box to see how the axle should be, remember to add on two centimetres from each end . . . alright?
Stacey: Axle, axle, these are the axles.

Mode E – Quarrelling   Talk that illustrates a clash of opinion in terms of action; seldom extended in nature. This can either be primitive; for example,
'No, you're not drawing the squares.'
or with motives; for example,
'That's not the way to do it . . . Because that's not what it says.'

Mode F – Primitive argument   Where talk takes the form of simple and opposing statements with no explicit reasoning or justification; it represents a move into abstract thought but is a parallel to quarrelling in action. For example,
a group are discussing the differences between two pieces of prose – one being in 'story' form, the other being a spoken account written down.

Lucy: The spoken version was boring but no-one else seems to think so.
Jo: I don't think it was boring. I don't think *boring*. It was different.
Robyn: I think it was different.
Jo: It was different but it wasn't boring.
Lucy: I think it was boring and not different.

Mode G – Collaboration   Where children discuss their work in terms of ideas or arguments which are logical and reasoned, sometimes with justification through the use of words such as 'since', 'then' or 'because'. For example,
children discussing poems make statements such as:

'I think it means he isn't getting any gold at all because he's not selling anything . . . That's what I think it is.'
'I think he's like the King of the Jungle. He sounds like it doesn't he?'

The children discussing the two pieces of prose (see mode F) make suggestions:

Robyn: I said the written one sounds more like a story.
Lucy: Yeah, same here. The second one sounds more like a story so I'm going to put, 'it had more details'.

Mode H – Genuine argument   For genuine argument to occur, demonstrations and logical solutions etc have to be made explicit. Use of 'because' and 'since' as logical connecters. The following example shows mode F moving into mode G.

Sophie: The ending was hopeless.
Holly: Was it? Do you think it was?
Luke: I liked the ending.
Sophie: It was too soppy though.
Luke: Too soppy?
Neil: Well I like it when they die at endings. It makes it a lot more funnier. It's a lot more good.
Holly: Well that's very nice, isn't it? [sarcastically!]
Neil: It's a lot more good – like – like – if I wrote a story I'd go 'as he swings his head with his sword' and stop the book there and they'd want to buy the next book wouldn't they?
Holly: No, probably wouldn't – because not many people like animals being killed.
Neil: They would.

The categorisation of the conversational modes into Action and Abstract is consistent with Piaget's model, as are the definitions of the two terms:

Action: talk related to the activity of the moment.
Abstract: talk no longer connected with the activity of the moment, but concerned with finding an explanation, reconstructing a story or a memory, discussing the order of events or the truth of a tale.

Before analysing the talk in terms of conversational modes, several prior categorisations were made (see Figure 3.3). The talk was first classified as task- or non-task-related. Task-related talk was then sub-divided, depending on its relevance to the task-demand. Talk not directly relevant would include that concerning the acquisition or manipulation of materials; for example, finding paper, sharpening pencils, etc – all necessary for task completion but not directly relevant to task-demand. Finally, a distinction was made between task-related talk that was socially oriented and that which was cognitively oriented. Socially oriented talk was that concerning the management of the group, whereas cognitively oriented talk related to the cognitive demand of the task. Once these distinctions had been made all task-related talk was then analysed for conversational mode. These classifications were carried out by trained observers, all of whom were qualified teachers. Training continued until inter-judge reliability was high (0.85).

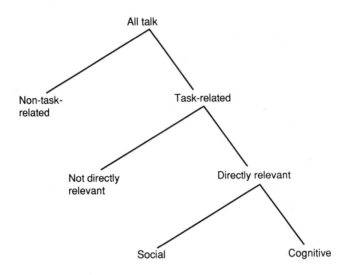

Figure 3.3 Classification system for all talk

Findings

(a) **Task-related talk.** Table 3.3 sets out the proportion of task-related talk in each curriculum area. The range of talk across groups is presented together with (for comparison purposes) the percentage of task-related talk in maths and language derived from an earlier study, when children were working on individual tasks within a group context. In general, task-related talk is very high, averaging 88 per cent, being highest in technology and computer tasks and lowest in language work. These levels achieved in co-operative groups can usefully be compared

Table 3.3 Task-related talk in curriculum areas

Curriculum	Task-related talk (%)	Range (%)	Task-related talk (Bennett *et al.*, 1984) (%)
Language	83	61–100	70
Maths	88	69–100	63
Technology	93	67–100	
Computers	99	98–100	
Average	88		66

Table 3.4 Types of task-related talk

Curriculum	Task-related talk		
	Not directly relevant (%)	Socially oriented (%)	Outcome oriented (%)
Language	15	13	72
Maths	11	13	76
Technology	10	8	82
Computers	5	5	90
Average	12	11	77

to the amounts of task-related talk found in the earlier study where children worked in groups but on individual tasks (Bennett *et al.*, 1984). It is clear that children in the co-operative settings demonstrate much greater involvement in their work, the average amount of task-related talk being 22 per cent higher.

Additionally, the amount of task-related talk not directly relevant to task completion was very low (see Table 3.4). The average was 12 per cent, being highest in English, and lowest in computer tasks. Socially oriented talk was similarly very low, averaging 11 per cent.

(b) Conversational modes. Table 3.5 presents the percentage of talk in the conversational modes in the four curriculum areas. Two patterns are of particular interest. First, the figure for maths in mode D (collaboration) is out of step with other curriculum areas; there is very

Table 3.5 Conversational modes in curriculum areas

Curriculum	Mode A (%)	B (%)	C (%)	D (%)	E (%)	F (%)	G (%)	H (%)
Language	7	11	26	32	5	4	14	2
Maths	9	50	26	5	9	0.5	–	–
Technology	1	20	17	56	2	0.5	3	–
Computers	–	–	16	70	5	3	5	–
Average	5	28	23	34	3	7	7	0.5

little collaboration. In English, technology and computer tasks the fact that the children are working co-operatively clearly shows in collaborative modes of talk. A possible explanation for this is in the group model chosen by all the teachers for maths work; that is, model 2 – jigsaw. This requires children to work individually initially, before bringing their work together for a common group outcome. There is thus a tendency for the talk to be more associative than collaborative.

The second pattern of interest is the amount of abstract talk generated by English tasks, amounting to 20 per cent of the total. This is in sharp contrast to maths tasks where it is near to zero, with a low proportion also in technology and computer tasks. The explanation for this contrasting pattern of action and abstract talk would seem to lie in the nature of the tasks set. Those assigned in maths, technology and for computers could be defined as 'action' tasks. Pupils are asked, for example, to make cubes, triangular prisms, carts that will roll down a slope, models for a fairground. These tasks are practical and therefore involve manipulation of materials. The children *have* to be involved in action in order to complete their tasks.

On the other hand, English tasks generally demand a different kind of activity. The children are asked to talk, to discuss and to make decisions unrelated to action. They are given problems to be solved verbally, tasks which ask them to look for meaning, to provide ideas, to compare and contrast. Alongside this, there is a demand to write or draw, sometimes as a group response, sometimes as individuals, in order to show what has been gained from the group discussion. Such tasks are characterised by a demand for 'abstract' thought, the action being secondary to this. So, for example, the whole group provide ideas for a single story, so that the emphasis is on creative thought; or the teacher provides a written or drawn stimulus for discussion, sometimes with questions to guide thinking – sometimes without. There is then a demand that this be completed by writing or by drawing.

(c) **Collaborative talk in action tasks.** As is apparent in Table 3.5, the largest proportion of talk is in mode D – collaboration. This collaborative talk can be either socially or cognitively oriented. The following examples have been selected to demonstrate the range and nature of this kind of talk.

A group of seven-years-olds are asked to make a set of cubes out of squared paper, each child contributing a cube of a different size, and the range of possibilities being limited by the size of paper. This leads to much interaction similar to:

Tania: Emily's doing the smallest.
James: I'm going to do the biggest.

Tania: I'm doing the smallest.
James: You're doing the biggest because you're the oldest . . .
        I'm doing the smallest even if you say I can't.
Tania: I'm doing the biggest one because I'm doing the best.

(Mode D – social)

Most of such talk is classified as 'Social' since it seems to revolve around vying for status within the group, but there is also a great deal which relates more closely to the cognitive demand:

Emily: I'm doing a five by five.
James: No, I'm doing five by five . . .
Tania: How are we going to make it anyway? I don't know anyway?
Lisa: You'll have to do another one like that won't you.
Emily: Uh uh. I did it wrong . . .
Lisa: I'm on my second. Is that perfect? That isn't perfect is it?
James: I've made mine and it goes just like a dice.
Lisa: Shall I screw this up and do it again?
Tania: Lisa are you doing the two side one? Hey, I know. You could do three lines.

(Mode D – cognitive
reference to dice – Mode G – cognitive)

This kind of interaction is very similar to that in a collaborative technology task where a group of seven- and eight-year-olds are asked to make a single cart, following precise instructions. They again discuss who can do what, sometimes arguing, sometimes resolving the problems associated with sharing materials:

Stacey: Can I saw the other part?
Heidi: Stacey can do another bit.
David: Wait a minute. I'm just marking it. I'm just marking it Stacey.
Heidi: Stacey's doing that part.
David: Stacey, quick! Sorry Paul, Stacey's doing it. Put it on this one for her . . . because you're not my best friend . . . wait a minute . . . there's plenty of sawing, look, these and these. Knocked it off. I'm clumsy. No don't.
Heidi: See if you can hold it there.
David: And properly.
Heidi: That's it isn't it.

(Mode D – social)

Ten minutes later:

   Heidi: We don't have to stick that down.
   David: No wait a minute. Scissors . . . scissors, pass me the scissors.
         Thanks. Cutting that bit of glue off, it's hanging off too
         much . . . you'll have to go that way . . . sticks to the box
         . . . it needs to anyway doesn't it?
   Heidi: Yes, but not yet because we are not sticking it . . . Now
         we need the triangles . . . we have to read the instructions
         . . . making the axle holders . . . no because we've already
         put . . . we need to get the triangles to strengthen the
         corners, stick the triangles in place, the picture will remind
         you if you have forgotten how to . . .
   David: No I'll use the scissors it's easier . . .
   Heidi: She's cutting out that . . .
   David: I know and I need to cut another one off there. They're
         not the same size . . . could have done with them a bit
         bigger.

                                        (Mode D – cognitive)

(d) Tasks that demand action and abstract talk. It is clear that decisions
about, and therefore talk about, action are important to practical tasks
and monopolise conversation. What is of particular interest is that for
tasks which combine action with abstract demands, talk related to
action continues to dominate. It seems as if, given the opportunity to
talk about action, the children will take it. Or it may be that, since an
end-product is always demanded by the teacher, the action required
for this is given the group's greatest attention.

Thus, in language lessons where there has been a real attempt
verbally to solve a problem as a group, talk relating to the writing up,
or to the drawing of ideas and meanings is always proportionately
higher.

An example of this is shown when a group of six- and seven-year-
olds are discussing a problem: which, out of a card, a cup of tea in
bed, or a bunch of flowers, would be the best way to surprise Mrs
Cook on her birthday? The children enter into this hypothetical
situation instantly, listening and replying to each other, making
decisions, justifying their responses:

   Andrew: Yes, but if we choose the flowers one she can put them
           in a vase.
   Louise: Yes, but they'll die so she won't keep them for very long.

Andrew: She will because . . .
Louise: They could be, they could be, those paper flowers couldn't they . . . because they last a long time.

(Mode H – cognitive)

Then:

Louise: I think the card.
Andrew: Yeah the card.
Louise: Because Mum can keep it for ages, she could always keep it forever . . . If we have a cup of tea Mum will drink it all.
Andrew: No she won't, she'll spill it.
Louise: In bed, she might spill the milk when she's pouring it in for her breakfast, so we'll have the card.
Donna: Yes.
Louise: Because, because, when the flowers are in the vase they could knock the vase over and the water would go over.

(Mode G – cognitive)

However, as soon as they begin to write and draw, it is this that retains their attention and action talk dominates thereafter. They talk about each other's drawings:

Philip: Is that a girl? Is that a girl? Actually this is a boy.
Louise: A boy?
Donna: That's a funny boy . . . that's got to be a girl.

(Mode D – cognitive)

They talk under their breath as they write. They ask each other what to do next:

Philip: What else shall I do Andrew?
Andrew: Don't ask me. Do the writing.
Philip: Oh, now I know.
Alan: Do the writing.
Philip: Right, I've got to do the writing.

(Mode D – cognitive)

Louise takes on a leadership role, especially helping Donna who finds the writing difficult:

Louise: Write <u>for</u> – for Mum.
Donna: F ... O ... R. No. There. OK?
Louise: F ... O ... R. For Mum. Can you write Mum there?
Andrew: Is that the way? Make a ... .
Philip: A ... C ... A ... R ... D.
Andrew: How do you write it? C ... A ... for? How do you write it ...?
Louise: No ... for Mum ... M ... F ... O ... R ...
Alan: C ... A ... R ... D ... F ... O ... R ... M ... U ... M ... for Mum.
Andrew: There, done it.

(Mode D – cognitive)

Louise then checks the group's writing and the children decide they have completed their task: high and low attainers have worked together; boys and girls have conversed readily with each other; they have solved all difficulties without bothering the teacher; and, most importantly, they have made a logical and justified choice from their three options, a choice which will then be explained to the rest of the class. Nevertheless, as soon as the action talk begins, further abstract talk is unlikely, for children of this age at least.

However, nine- and ten-year-olds respond in a slightly different way to a similar task. They are given a long poem which is read both with the teacher and by the group. The children are asked to draw individual posters to illustrate the poem and told also that they may be challenged about its meaning. Throughout their work, the children move across many modes of talk; the action and abstract modes are intermingled. Each drawing needs to reflect the description and sense of the poem, and the children thus search for meaning as this becomes important to their illustration:

Mary Anne: No I'm not. I'm sitting him down with his hands over his face crying. He's an old man isn't he?
Samantha: I dunno. Yes I think ... Does it say old? Does it say man?
Mary Anne: An old ... yeah ... It says 'the old King of the Makers.'
Samantha: If it says 'King' it must be a man.

(Mode H – cognitive)

Much of the group's talk refers to action, as in the following discussion about their drawings.

Mary Anne: Look Samantha! Look Samantha at my palm tree.

Samantha:	What?
Mary Anne:	Silly, isn't it? Doesn't look like a palm tree at all, does it?
Neil:	Is that a little bull frog?
Matthew:	Glow worms!
Neil:	I'm going to put the sea in my desert.
Samantha:	I'm drawing palm trees.

(Mode D – cognitive)

Yet the children return to abstract talk when they need to know the meaning of a word:

Matthew:	. . . clayman. What's a clayman?
Mary Anne:	How the hell should I know what a clayman is . . . A clayman is, a clayman is a clayman.
Matthew:	No but you wouldn't find a clayman in the jungle.
Samantha:	The cayman not a clayman.
Mary Anne:	How should I know what a cayman is?
Matthew:	Well go up and ask.

(Mode H – cognitive)

Teachers were occasionally concerned that talk in abstract tasks was not extensive or fluent. However, in these data, the most faltering discussions are characterised by talk in modes F, G and H; that is, where real problem-solving is tackled through talk. It would thus be unfair to compare this hard won, albeit faltering progression with the often free-flowing spontaneity of talk relating to action.

Classroom processes

(a) **Managing time.** We argued in Chapter 1 that too much of the teacher's time is eaten up by responding to large numbers of pupil demands, and that this time could be more profitably used on other things such as assessment and diagnosis. We further argued that the best way forward was to amend styles of classroom management. In particular, we hypothesised that time could be created in classrooms where co-operative grouping was being used, by the teacher devolving to the group some of her authority. In other words, children would not be allowed to make requests of the teacher until all the possibilities of finding an answer had been exhausted in the group.

In order to test out the effectiveness of this approach the 15 teachers monitored the demands of their pupils prior to, and after, they had

Table 3.6 Pattern of pupil demands before and after devolution of responsibility

	Before		After	
Total demands	Average demands per lesson	Demands per category (%)	Average demands per lesson	Demands per category (%)
1 Instruction	2.0	5	0.8	19
2 Presentation	0	0	0.2	5
3 Management procedure	4.0	10	1.1	27
4 Management behaviour	1.5	4	0	0
5 Evaluation interim	12.0	31	1.0	23
6 Evaluation final	7.5	19	0.1	2
7 Transitions	5.0	13	0.1	1
8 Spellings	2.5	6	0.3	7
9 Materials	4.0	10	0.6	13
10 Routine	0	0	0.2	4
Total	38.5	100	4.4	100

set up cooperative groupwork, using the observation schedule in Figure 3.1. Table 3.6 shows the pattern of change which occurred. The average number of demands fell dramatically, from an average of over 38 per lesson to less than five. The type of demand also changed. Before devolution, almost two-thirds of the requests were to do with evaluation or transitions. After devolution, these comprised only one-quarter of requests. It would appear that the group can, in fact, handle most of the demands that individual pupils would usually make of teachers. The increase of instructional requests from one-twentieth to one-fifth of the total demonstrates that children are involved in 'higher level' demands on the teacher's time rather than with more mundane requests.

The types of help needed will, of course, vary enormously, but even young children can monitor the correctness or quality of each other's work, make decisions about materials, layout, sequence of work, and so on. The kind of task given to children is also likely to have an impact on the types of demand on the teacher.

One teacher described how demand patterns can be almost instantly changed by asking children to refer to their group rather than to her. When she monitored two sessions she found that:

'a total of 27 demands were made upon me during the space of 30 minutes during an integrated day. Of these 27 demands almost half, 13, in fact, were demands for me to evaluate partly completed or completed tasks. All demands were made by individual children needing help or reassurance about their own work.

During the second demand session there were far fewer demands made upon my time. During a half-hour period there were only five requests made for interim evaluation, ie, "Is this alright?"'

These children were aged seven to eight and were able to adjust their behaviour immediately when requested to do so. Of particular importance is their teacher's claim that the quality of work was exceptionally good during this lesson, with the suggestion that most of the previous demands really had been unnecessary.

In a series of four lessons, another teacher of six- to eight-year-olds found that demands dropped significantly, and, as illustrated below, many of the demands that were made *did* require her presence.

'Although the children had "spelling partners" and experienced encouragement to co-operate before the project began, there were 12 demands on my time in the first session.

In the second session there were three pupil demands, one came from Phillip, the youngest member of the highlighted group. His paper had fallen on the floor, and he came to tell me he had no paper. One group leader was unsure of the task procedure, and one other child asked for the curtains to be drawn, because the sun was in her eyes.

In the third session one child had a nosebleed, and there were no other demands on my time.

In the fourth session, I walked around the classroom monitoring the groups, and near the end of the lesson went to a group where one child was upset.

During the project the number of pupil demands fell away to almost zero. The children were clearly able to work well at their tasks without constant recourse to me and they showed clear benefits from the attitudes and skills they had acquired.'

It is clear from Table 3.6 that these are not isolated cases of substantial change in pupil behaviour; they serve as illustrations of the general trend. Teacher comments bear this out: 'Much more time was available to teach rather than to deal with many matters which can be peer assisted.' Another reinforced this, stating that, 'It is a management method that really frees the teacher, and would enable her to carry out the profiling, observation and testing jobs.' So much time was freed in some classrooms that the teachers began to feel guilty at not being rushed off their feet. 'I found it very satisfying teaching in this way because the children were so involved in their work. It gave me a lot of free time . . . At times this made me feel that I was not doing my job.' Although some of the teachers had initially felt anxious about devolving responsibility to the groups, they found that their concerns were not in reality justified; the many examples of children talking that are given throughout this book bear out this lack of need for concern, for pupils tackle their co-operative tasks in serious and responsible ways. One teacher made useful distinctions between two types of demand, discussing how classroom management can influence them. She wrote:

'We can split the demand categories into two, those demands that can be called routine: transitions, spellings, materials, routine, procedure and behaviour; and those to do with the process of the task: instruction, presentation, evaluation and sharing findings. In the area of routine it is easier to 'teach' cooperative behaviour as concrete strategies can be used. For example, to ease transitions between tasks, it is common practice to build up a bank of ongoing activities; for spelling, clear spelling strategies can be built into the classroom practice; for materials, examples of establishing cooperative behaviour in this area are not difficult to find and the nature of the primary classroom is such that materials can be stored in an accessible way; for procedure, the clarity of the teacher's demands and the understanding by the group of the extent of 'ownership' of an activity will ensure that the group is independent. Routine and behaviour demands reflect class ethos and the quality and engagement of the task.

The more challenging areas to tackle are those of instruction, presentation, evaluation and shared findings. Here we must pose questions of the nature: can you teach explanation? How can questioning be encouraged? Can you model questions of the 'how' and 'why' type? And if the answers are positive, how much effect does this have on collaborative learning?'

This same teacher also shows how, during a series of twelve lessons, she was able to use her newly acquired time (Table 3.7). Much of the time was spent in 'walkabout' which involved monitoring, intervention and the sharing of ideas with the class, groups and individuals. From the teacher's point of view, one of the greatest advantages was that

Table 3.7 Teacher activities during a series of groupwork lessons

Teacher's Activities	1	2	3	4	5	6	7	8	9	10	11	12
Observation	√	√	√	√	√	√	√	√	√	√	√	√
Conference with individuals			√					√			√	
Conference with groups						√			√	√		
Whole class instruction				√	√	√				√	√	
Sharing books with individuals				√	√		√					√
'Jobs'					√				√			√
Planning							√					
Walkabout					√				√	√	√	

there was time to observe, to interact and so gain some measure of the learning demands made by the tasks set. An increase in time also allowed open-ended questions to be asked and responded to. This in turn gave time for the formative type of assessment that the National Curriculum demands.

(b) **Teacher responses.** A major aim of the study was to ascertain what issues arose in the classroom as a consequence of setting up co-operative groups. The most crucial factors in this process were of course the teachers. We therefore asked each teacher to produce a reflective account of their experiences, giving their general impressions as well as considering specific areas of concern. What follows is a summary of these accounts. None of the teachers had used co-operative groups in the past, and readily admitted that they had previously had no policy or rationale for their groupwork. They were typical of most teachers in having set up groups, but then used them purely for individual tasks and outcomes.

The ways they had composed their groups were varied. Forty per cent tended to use ability groups for maths work, but otherwise used friendship groups, whereas the rest used a variety of mixed ability and friendship groups.

All the teachers had expressed a positive view about trying 'proper' co-operative grouping involving mixed ability groups and low levels of intervention. Indeed, half of them set up informal training sessions for themselves and the children. In some classrooms this was simply a statement of the rules governing groupwork, in others the children themselves came to conclude that groupwork would be beneficial because 'sharing individual ideas usually resulted in better ideas . . . they also decided on appropriate ways of imposing sanctions and what was and was not, suitable behaviour.' Another teacher concentrated on removing herself from the children's demands and 'actively encouraged the children to use each other as a resource.'

Without exception, the teachers found co-operative grouping easier to implement than they had imagined. 'I was pleasantly surprised at how easy the sessions were'; 'The children performed in a more business-like way than I'd expected.' All stated that the children enjoyed this way of working, had responded well and were enthusiastic about continuing to work in this way. Indeed most were surprised at how well their children had co-operated. 'I was agreeably surprised to find that the children were in fact able to use each other and help each other more than I had realised.'

Several teachers pointed out that seating patterns and leadership were important ingredients of group success. One noted, for example, that the less able should be seated between those of average or above average ability so as to seek their help rather than being physically isolated at the edge of the group.

Many teachers noted that successful groups were those in which one child took on a leadership role. Although in the majority of cases this was a high attainer, this was not always so. These leaders, commented their teachers, assumed the teaching role and verbally encouraged the group to complete the work, and were only prepared to let 'silly behaviour go so far.'

It is interesting to note that where children worked in groups composed of both boys and girls, it was reported that boys tended to take the dominant role. The girls seemed to accept this and worked happily together. This was particularly evident in computer tasks. In one class, the teacher carried out an additional study into the use of the keyboard by boys and girls. He observed pupils aged between five and nine in mixed-sex groups of three as they came to the computer. He noted that, out of 81 children observed, 'only two extremely bright and confident girls managed to get control.'

Teachers also noted that disruptive children 'settled down well, without all the usual arguments and disruptive behaviour' and that children with behavioural difficulties had responded well to co-operative groupwork.

One of the over-riding successes of setting up groups was the benefit observed for lower attaining children. All but one teacher commented on the surprising contributions of these pupils: 'they took a substantial part in conversation'; 'I was surprised at the extent that the less able contributed to the group's success.' This involvement was a particular bonus to those teachers who had previously used ability groups for some curriculum areas. One talked of the problem the lower attaining group had been for her in the past as they were very demanding of her time, and, because they worked in isolation from the rest of the class, fell further and further behind. She said that with co-operative groupwork, these children were encouraged by the higher attainers and did more work as the pace of the group was faster, and that for her 'it was a relief to split up this lower ability group who were constantly demanding my attention.'

Another teacher told a similar story. She found that one of the repercussions of co-operative groupwork was that whereas the lower attaining children had tended to sit together in the past, after the groupwork sessions they often sat 'with higher ability children who took them under their wings.' She felt this was of great benefit to these low achievers.

Against this very positive picture of implementation must be placed the concerns of two teachers who, although stating that their children had performed very well, were a little disappointed at the amount of help that the children had given to each other. They believed one of two things had caused this, either a lack of training, or the nature of the task worked on. Similarly, a teacher who was concerned about her lower attainers said that they often seemed unable to be an integral part of the activity, again a reference to the nature of the task.

Choosing appropriate tasks for co-operative working proved to be one of the most difficult aspects of the implementation. Half of the sample felt that they had either made a poor choice of task or that they could have improved on it. In the maths/technology area, the two teachers who used computer tasks felt that the adventure game used did not produce high quality language. A teacher who had designed a maths task felt that it 'should have included a further element of problem solving which would possibly have encouraged the group towards higher levels of thinking.' Another felt that although the task matched the children's abilities it was a poor co-operative task because it was possible to complete it with minimal dialogue. Significant, perhaps, is that this was one of the two teachers who was disappointed with the amount of helping behaviour. The other disappointed teacher had chosen a language task which he later argued was inappropriate because it relied on visual skills and focussed on writing rather than co-operating.

Overall, task design proved a difficult area. As one teacher wrote, 'designing and presenting the task is one of the biggest problems of cooperative groupwork.' Echoing this, another concluded: 'there is a need for a range of suitable activities to be designed for co-operative groupwork.'

Clearly, then, the quality of the task has an important impact on the quality of the work, and this is reflected in the teachers' comments about children's completed work. Seventy per cent of the teachers were very positive, incorporating such statements as, 'there was a dramatic increase in the amount of discussion, suggestion, testing, inferring and drawing informed conclusions'; and 'they generally produced work of a better standard.' One noted that there was evidence of 'rich mathematical language' and another said her children's work was 'more thorough and presented well' when it was produced as a co-operative effort. Finally, one of the teachers gave this enthusiastic account, which arose after a language session on poetry:

'I was amazed at the sensitivity and perception of the meanings in the poem. I was delighted that this whole assignment had developed the conditions for such high quality learning to take place. Children were thinking and reflecting their views and not a teacher's ... The group was ... a safe environment in which to test hypotheses and try out new ideas. The talk I was involved in was as an equal and I learned more about the poem from the children than I would have on my own.'

In the main, the teachers who were not as happy with the outcomes were those who were unhappy with the tasks they had designed. Thus one, who, although 'impressed by some of the exchanges of language', felt that the quality and range were disappointing, also felt that his task had been inappropriate. Another said that this was probably because the task chosen by her allowed a look-and-copy approach.

Perhaps the most significant comments come from the two teachers involved with computer tasks. One thought he would get 'all sorts of interesting conversations' and the other had expected the computer task to 'stimulate and extend the children's language', but both were disappointed. The latter teacher found that 'the majority of the talk was operational, related solely to the functioning of the computer and the programme' and the former found similarly that 'most of the talk is procedural and a great percentage is merely collaborative reading what is on the screen.' There was no evidence, he said, of 'collaborative thinking.'

(c) **Sex differences.** Although in our previous research on groups we have found little difference between boys and girls in their type and frequency of talk, the comments of the teachers on group leadership, particularly about the dominance by boys, led us to undertake a series of analyses to ascertain if differences did indeed exist. Boys and girls were first contrasted on types of task-related talk, and then on modes of talk, before considering whether modes of talk varied in groups containing different proportions of boys and girls. These analyses were carried out in exactly the same way as those reported earlier in this chapter.

First, boys and girls were compared on the amounts of task-related talk in each curriculum area. This is shown in Table 3.8. In language tasks boys and girls do not differ in type of talk, and the proportions of their time spent on task is both high and very similar. However, it is not as high as in maths and technology tasks. Here girls spend more time on task than boys. Their patterns of talk are also slightly different, girls devoting more of their talk to social outcomes and boys talking more about materials and the like.

But does this pattern imply that their modes of talk are the same? In order to answer this question, all of the children's talk was classified into the eight modes of conversation. The results are shown in Table 3.9, not in the eight modes, but grouped into three broader modes in order to show the patterns more clearly. Thus modes A and B are joined to create a category of 'non-collaborative' talk; modes C, D and E are joined to make a category of 'collaborating-in-action' talk; and

Table 3.8 Task-related talk: boys and girls

	On-task (%)	Cognitive (%)	Social (%)	Not central (%)
Language				
Boys	82	73	13	14
Girls	84	72	13	15
Maths/technology				
Boys	86	79	8	13
Girls	93	80	12	8

Table 3.9 Modes of talk in language and maths/technology tasks

	Non-collaborative	Collaborating in action	Collaborating in abstract
Language			
Boys	16	69	14
Girls	19	53	28
Maths/technology			
Boys	44	53	2
Girls	34	64	2

F, G and H are joined to create 'collaborating-in-abstract' talk. Table 3.9 shows very interesting differences between boys and girls in both areas of the curriculum. It will be recalled that abstract talk was far more prevalent in language tasks. This pattern clearly shows again here, but of further importance is the fact that the girls spoke twice as much as boys in the abstract modes. Boys' talk was more clearly grounded in action. Although very little abstract talk was evident in maths/technology tasks, here too girls' talk was more developed than boys. Girls also provided the most collaboration-in-action talk, although just over a third of their talk was non-collaborative. However, this is in comparison to the boys' talk – almost half of which was non-collaborative.

The patterns of talk presented in Tables 3.8 and 3.9 are based on the total number of words spoken by boys and girls, irrespective of the composition of the group in which they worked. However, the groups varied in the number of boys and girls they contained, and this led us to question whether the composition of the group had any impact on the modes of talk used. For example, did the finding that girls spoke twice as much abstract talk as boys hold true if there were more, or fewer, girls in the group than boys?

The analyses shown in Tables 3.10 and 3.11 present modes of talk in relation to three types of group composition; ie, where there were equal numbers of boys and girls, where there were more girls than boys, and where there were more boys than girls. Language tasks are considered first. A very interesting pattern emerges from the language tasks. The pattern of talk is similar for both sexes when groups are made up of equal numbers of boys and girls, and where there are more girls than boys; that is, less of the girls' talk is non-collaborative, there is less sharing-in-action talk, but almost twice as much collaboration-

Table 3.10 Types of talk in different types of group: language tasks

| Mode of talk | Group type | | | | | |
| | Equal boys and girls | | More girls than boys | | More boys than girls | |
	b	g	b	g	b	g
Non-collaborative (%)	28	17	19	15	13	25
Collaborating in action (%)	53	48	55	44	74	66
Collaborating in abstract (%)	19	37	25	42	13	9

Table 3.11 Types of talk in different types of group: maths/technology tasks

| Mode of talk | Group type | | | | | |
| | Equal boys and girls | | More girls than boys | | More boys than girls | |
	b	g	b	g	b	g
Non-collaborative (%)	47	35	35	30	74	56
Collaborating in action (%)	53	65	65	67	26	44

in-abstract talk. In groups where there are more boys than girls, however, the picture changes dramatically. Here, twice as much of the girls' talk is non-collaborative and, more significantly, they speak less in the abstract modes. The finding that girls' abstract talk is substantially lower in groups where they are outnumbered by boys, if replicated, could be of great importance for teachers in deciding who should sit with whom. Unfortunately, we cannot back up this finding in the maths/technology area because there is so little abstract talk. Table 3.11 shows the findings from this area. Here there are no differences in the tiny amount of abstract talk recorded (less than 2 per cent); for this reason, abstract talk is ignored. Here, too, there is clear evidence that talk is substantially different in groups where there are more boys than girls. In this type of group, non-collaborative talk is substantially higher for both sexes, with a corresponding diminution in collaboration in action talk for both.

Tables do not take into account how much boys and girls talk in these different groupings, simply the mode. In order to take both quantity of talk and mode into account requires a 'fair shares' analysis, and an example is shown in Appendix A. As will be seen, the resultant patterns are very similar, but they do allow an elaboration of the findings related to the nature of girls' abstract talk in different types of group. What Table 3.10 indicates is that the proportion of girls' talk in the collaborating-in-abstract category is much higher than boys when they are in groups where the number of boys is the same or fewer. When girls are in groups with more boys, the proportion of their abstract talk is considerably less.

What Table A.1 (see Appendix A) further shows is that girls actually speak more in the former settings and speak less in the latter. In other words, it is not just that the proportion of their talk in the abstract category is lower, they actually speak fewer words.

These patterns are provocative and argue for further work on a more representative sample of group types.

Summary

The analyses of group talk confirmed the findings of our earlier study (Bennett and Cass, 1988) that task-related talk is very high in co-operative groups. The major extension here has been the consideration of modes of task-related talk, and how these change in relation to task-demand. The findings clearly show that action talk predominates in all the curriculum areas studied, appearing to be a direct response to the demands in the tasks set. Where abstract demands are made, as in some English tasks, abstract talk occurs.

What was surprising, and perhaps disconcerting, was the lack of abstract demands in maths, science and technology tasks. However, the teacher does of course have the opportunity to organise clashes of opinion in tasks which are otherwise action oriented via class discussion and evaluation.

Generally, the teachers were extremely pleased with the outcomes of their implementation of co-operative groups. Several were astonished at the decline in pupil demands on them, releasing them for more important work such as monitoring and assessing. The setting up of the groups had been easier than they had expected, and the quality of the pupil's work had, in their view, improved irrespective of the ability of the child. There were, nevertheless, difficulties, the prime one being the design of tasks suitable for co-operative working.

Finally, sex differences were considered in relation to group composition. The finding that being a girl in groups containing more boys depressed not only the amount of their talk, but also the proportion of it which was of a higher level, is worrying and requires further study.

4 Designing tasks: Cognitive aspects

Introduction

In 1980, Galton *et al.* complained both about the lack of co-operative groupwork in our classrooms and about the lack of research on its implementation.

> 'In particular no serious attention appears to have been given, even in relation to the teaching of science and mathematics, to the key issue as to how the teacher, responsible for the work of a whole class (perhaps split into four, five or more groups), is to ensure that each group, engaged on co-operative tasks involving discussion and the use of materials and apparatus, is effectively and meaningfully occupied.'

They continue by emphasising the difficulties for both children and teachers if they are to be seriously involved in the development of co-operative learning, and perhaps thereby suggest an explanation for its lack of presence in our classrooms.

> 'To think out, provide materials for, and set up a series of group tasks having the characteristics just described in the different subject areas which comprise a modern curriculum would in itself clearly be a major undertaking, even if use is made of relevant curriculum development projects. To monitor the subsequent group activities; to be ready and able to intervene in the work of each group when this is educationally necessary or desirable; this also would clearly be a major undertaking for the teacher requiring, as a first condition, a high degree of involvement by the pupils in their tasks and so a high level of responsible behaviour.'

For the pupils to gain from such work also certainly requires the development of a number of social as well as cognitive, skills; a degree of tolerance and mutual understanding, the ability to articulate a point of view, to engage in discussion, reasoning, probing and questioning. Such skills are not in themselves innate, they have to be learnt and so taught.'

Ten years later, despite a great deal more interest in groupwork, and the National Curriculum requirements for its use, we still have no sure-fire rules for success in implementation. Indeed, the more is known, the more the problematic nature and complexities of co-operative work become apparent. Slavin (1983) raises some of the issues:

'It is easy to criticize the instructional system used in traditional classrooms. However, proposing systematic alternatives is not so easy. In the case of applying the principles of cooperation to replace the competitive incentive structure and individualistic task structure of the traditional classroom, the most direct method would be to assign students to small groups, let them work together, and praise them based on their group product. This would solve many of the problems of the traditional classroom. However, it could create a long list of new problems. What would keep the co-operative groups from turning out like those laboratory groups in which one or two students end up doing most of the work? Why should students help each other learn – why should they care how their classmates are doing? What would keep the more able students from belittling the contributions of their lower-performing peers? How in fact could low-achieving students contribute anything important to their groups? How can students focus their studying activities to achieve the greatest possible learning for all group members? What kinds of learning materials and activities should be used with co-operative methods?'

It is issues such as these that we investigate in the next four chapters. Enabling children to work successfully together for both social and cognitive gain is not straightforward and it is not possible to advocate any single, specific way ahead. For this reason, we investigate aspects of research which we believe to be informative and useful and, in particular, look at evidence of the ways in which teachers use groupwork in their own classrooms, how they plan and organise, how they set up tasks, monitor and assess. In this way we provide insight and guidance to allow informed decision-making on future classroom practice.

Designing tasks

The design of tasks for co-operative groupwork is an area that is crucial and yet is one that has received little attention from researchers either in America or Europe. We have already discussed two major aspects of task design in Chapter 3, as well as the different kinds of impact they may have on the group:

(a) the cognitive demand of the task – which relates to the content and structure of the activity, and is reflected in the type of talk – that is, whether it is abstract in kind or whether it is dominated by the action, or activity, of the children. At present, this seems to be mostly determined by the curriculum area undertaken.

(b) the social demand of the task – which relates closely to the demands for co-operation within a specific activity and which again is reflected in the type of talk.

Figure 4.1 separates out these two features:

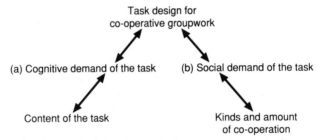

Figure 4.1 Cognitive and social demands for co-operative tasks

Cowie and Ruddock (1989) emphasise the need for this split:

'If group work is to take its proper place within a common repertoire of ways of learning, then teachers must distinguish two different justifications – the personal/social and the intellectual.'

They believe that teachers are more prepared at present to accept the need for groupwork in social terms, but are less likely to consider the intellectual possibilities and advantages. The National Oracy Project (NOP, 1990) also takes up a similar distinction. They state:

'There are three aspects of talking and listening which, though interlinked, can usefully be distinguished to explore a complicated concept. These are: the **social** aspect of talk, concerned with people getting along with each other; the **communicative** aspect of referring to talk as a means of transferring meaning between people; and the **cognitive** aspect, emphasizing talk as a means of learning.'

They also provide a diagrammatic representation of the relationship between these aspects (Figure 4.2). However this diagram inevitably simplifies something which is indeed more complex, for the content of the task may have a greater or lesser impact on the need for co-operation; or the cognitive and social demands may at times be one and the same and at other times be clearly separate and identifiable.

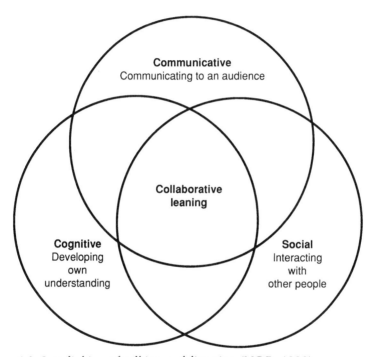

Figure 4.2 Interlinking of talking and listening (NOP, 1990)

If we now link our own diagram for task design for co-operative groupwork (Figure 4.1) to an actual task, it will give an idea of how each of the features within it can be developed and how they are inter-related. As an example, take the statement of attainment (level 5) from the English 'Speaking and Listening' targets: 'plan and participate in a presentation; eg, of the outcome of a group activity, a poem, story, dramatic scene or play.' This statement was interpreted by the teacher in terms of children participating in a presentation of a radio news programme.

One way of fulfilling this demand in terms of a group activity is to set up a 'jigsaw' task; that is, children work at individual items for the news programme, but must plan together and must fit the individual items together to make a coherent whole. In this case, the teacher chose a cognitive demand in terms of a statement of attainment and then decided on the way in which she wanted pupils to work at it, opting for a jigsaw method. It would, however, be possible to decide on a method of working in groups first of all (say, jigsaw) and then plan the cognitive demand to fit this social demand. Either way, the two are closely linked.

The next stage for the teacher is to enable the children to fulfil her plan. At the implementation stage, the pupils will have to make decisions about, for example, the new material to be used and the style of presentation, and they will have to write the items or reports. Since this is set up as a jigsaw task, it is important that some work is undertaken as a group and some is individual. Pupils will, therefore, have to decide on who does what within the group and who writes which report, they will have to check that individual work reaches the desired standard and that they pay attention to each others' ideas, and

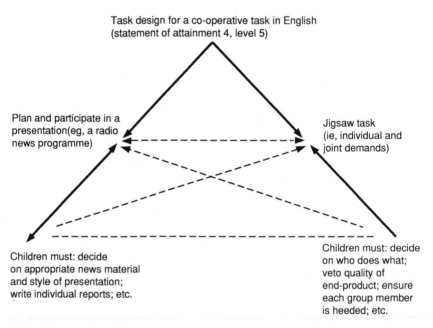

Task design for a co-operative task in English
(statement of attainment 4, level 5)

Plan and participate in a presentation(eg, a radio news programme)

Jigsaw task
(ie, individual and joint demands)

Children must: decide on appropriate news material and style of presentation; write individual reports; etc.

Children must: decide on who does what; veto quality of end-product; ensure each group member is heeded; etc.

Figure 4.3 Planning for cognitive and social demands

they will have to organise the actual presentation together. Once again, the cognitive demand and the social demand are closely linked; both dictate the way in which children will be expected to operate.

Figure 4.3 represents these stages of task design and demonstrates the links between them. Even in this form, it is only a skeleton plan and a teacher would have to make further decisions; for example, about how to ensure that both cognitive and social demands were understood by the children, or about the kinds of materials that would need to be provided to enable pupils to work in this way.

The cognitive demand of the task and the social demand of the task are now considered in turn in this and the following chapter. Despite this split being somewhat artificial, it is useful to consider each aspect separately.

The cognitive demand of the task

All those who write about co-operative groupwork make it clear that the tasks given to pupils are all-important. Slavin (1983), for example, states that:

> 'It is not enough to simply tell students to co-operate. A program based on co-operation among students must be "engineered", both to solve the problems inherent in co-operation itself and to adapt co-operative activities to the needs and limitations of the typical classroom.'

Yet in a series of worksheets produced for his research in the USA, he uses questions which focus on prerequisite knowledge or narrow pre-determined experiences. For example,

(a)   the capital of Canada is . . .
(b)   He sat . . . through the trial. (calm/calmly)
(c)   A combination of calcium and chlorine would be written:
       ca cl / CaCl / CaCl / Ca Cl

There may be a place for this kind of activity in our classrooms, but it seems likely that, in Britain, there would be more sympathy for an approach which favours cognitive development promoted by the task itself, for example, by problem-solving rather than the learning of facts. Thus it is the task that is expected to provide intrinsic motivation.

Another American researcher, Cohen (1986), favours a cognitive approach. She explains how 'thinking' is central to effective groupwork, and how this 'thinking' is dependent on whether the children are well-prepared for the task in terms of prerequisite skills.

'Groupwork can be more effective than traditional methods for gaining a proper understanding of abstract concepts . . . The learning task should require conceptual thinking rather than learning to apply a rule or memorization.'

However, she stresses that if such an approach is to be worthwhile:

'The group must have the resources to complete the assignment successfully. These included intellectual skills, relevant information and properly prepared task instructions.'

The kind of groupwork tasks chosen by the teachers in our research and tasks outlined by other researchers (see below) show that this kind of approach is widely accepted in Britain, and that children are introduced to activities which encourage them to apply and use pre-existing knowledge, skills and experiences.

This is possible with even the youngest of school children. For example, a reception class are divided into groups in order to answer the question: 'What can you see, smell, hear and touch around the school?' The teacher states: 'The task not only practises attainment targets in the National Curriculum, but its design was to consolidate the work already covered in topic work on the five senses. It is therefore an enrichment task – a task which demands the use of familiar knowledge, concepts and skills in unfamiliar contexts.'

There are several features of task design which have attracted researchers and educationists, and which have an impact on the cognitive demand:

- the form of the task
- problem-solving tasks
- 'loose' and 'tight' frameworks
- pupil-planning.

Each of these is considered in turn. However, although it is possible to separate out these features, they are not necessarily discrete; indeed there is a great deal of overlap between them.

The form of the task

Cowie and Rudduck (1989) point out that groupwork can take many forms in the classroom: their examples of tasks apply particularly to secondary-age pupils, but the general principles apply, and the descriptions are clear.

'Group work has many guises: in classrooms it mainly takes the following forms.

Discussion: here a larger group of pupils and their teacher, or a smaller group of pupils without their teacher's constant presence, work to share understandings and ideas. The focus may be the interpretation of something which is ambiguous (a picture, a poem, etc), the sharing of experiences, the pooling of ideas, or the eliciting of opinions on an issue of common concern. Discussions may lead to enhanced individual understanding, or they may require negotiation in the interests of arriving at a group consensus.

Problem-solving tasks: these usually depend on the discussion of alternatives as a medium for constructive interaction. Often the same task is set simultaneously to a number of small groups of three or four pupils, and there may be a final review of solutions with mutual criticism. Alternatively, an overall problem might be identified as a framework in which groups of pupils work on different aspects of the task and the different contributions are then brought together and reviewed.

Production tasks: these are slightly different from problem-solving tasks in that there is usually a concrete outcome: that is, pupils might be working in teams to produce, say, a film, with one team responsible for the research, one for the technical work, one for the programme sequencing, etc. Or pupils might work in small groups to design and produce, say, a bookstand that even if only partially full holds the books upright! Here, like the problem-solving task, there may be a communal, whole group review of the progress of different bits of the jig-saw, or there may be a comparison of products and even a judgement as to the best.'

In the lessons reviewed throughout this book, all of these three forms of groupwork are apparent. However, we consider that all three kinds of task above are actually problem-solving tasks. In all the activities we investigate in classrooms, the children are faced with problems, whether it be in terms of developing deeper understanding during a discussion or in terms of making individual or group products; all the tasks we observed demanded 'thinking'. 'Problem-solving' in the narrow sense as used by Cowie and Rudduck is a useful framework for a particular kind of problem-solving activity dependent on discussing alternative propositions; it could also be viewed as a specific form of discussion task (and one that is particularly successful as we shall outline later). Further, although we do not have any examples of 'alternative possibilities' being used for production tasks, it seems a potentially useful idea.

Thus, we recommend that all groupwork tasks should be dependent on an element of problem-solving (and this is considered in more detail in the next section) and that a useful distinction can be made between 'discussion' tasks and 'production' tasks.

Our distinction between abstract and action tasks can be easily applied to these two forms: discussion, not having an end-product, leads to abstract talk, whereas production tasks promote talk relating to the action necessary to achieve the end-product. Again it does not mean that abstract talk cannot occur in an action context, or that children do not think in abstract ways, but that their talk is dominated by the action. However, to complicate matters, teachers also set tasks for which an element of production is necessary, but where their major demand is for abstract discussion. This feature of groupwork will be enlarged on later in the chapter, where we will look in more detail at an example of this kind of task: children are drawing posters to illustrate a poem (a production task) but the emphasis is on gaining understanding of the poem through group discussion (a discussion task).

Cowie and Rudduck also state that, 'What matters is that teachers frame the task in ways that support the distinctive potential of learning through groupwork.' Their forms of groupwork do allow a certain insight into appropriate kinds of task, but still leave a great deal to the imagination of the teacher as to how this potential can be achieved.

Problem-solving tasks

Problem-solving is a much-used term, but one that is hard to define. In order to provide a better description of the kinds of activity which teachers consider to be centred on 'problem-solving', a selection of tasks and children's responses to them are outlined below. The successful tasks always contain an element of decision-making to be undertaken by the group, but there are many ways in which this can be set up within an activity.

(a) **Discussion of alternatives.**

Andrew   Philip

Louise | Five children discuss the choice of a birthday gift. End-product: a decision to be shared with the class. | Alan

Donna

A group of six- and seven-year-olds are discussing a problem: which choice – of a card, a cup of tea in bed, or a bunch of flowers – would be the best way to surprise Mrs Cook on her birthday? This is, according to the Cowie and Rudduck definition, a typical 'problem-solving' task, since the options are limited and the discussion is of alternatives. The children are given pictures with written reminders of the choices, and may choose their own solution. They are asked to have a good reason for their choice. The children enter into this hypothetical situation instantly.

Andrew: Yes, but if we choose the flowers one she can put them in a vase.

Philip: What if we . . . what if we choose them?

Alan: I think . . . I think . . .

Louise: Yes, but they'll die so she won't keep them for very long.

Andrew: She will because . . . Yes, yes. Or but they could be wrapped in paper.

Louise: They could be, they could be, those paper flowers couldn't they . . .? Because they last a long time.

Andrew: Yes, I think . . .

Donna: Yes, there . . .

Louise: I think the card.

Donna: Yes, but . . .

Andrew: Yeah, the card.

Louise: Because Mum can keep it for ages, she could always keep it forever . . . if we have a cup of tea Mum will drink it all.

Andrew: No she won't, she'll spill it.

Donna: Andrew, that was a brilliant idea.

Louise: In bed, she might spill the milk when she's pouring it in for her breakfast, so we'll have the card.

Donna: Yes.

Louise: Because, because, when the flowers are in the vase they could knock the vase over and the water would go over . . . Yes. We shall have that one . . . yes?

Philip: No. Shall we have that? [pointing to the pictures.]

Louise: So we're having this one. No, we're having this one. They should make Mum a card. Yes?

Donna: I think they should. Me too.

At this point, the group seem to have reached a consensus. They now each have to write down their group's decision and then report on this to the other groups during a whole-class discussion. The decision-making process took less than three minutes and the writing a little longer, despite the fact that their teacher had put a good deal of time into planning and preparing the task. Although this balance of preparation to activity might suggest a poor use of teacher time, the quality of the response seems well worth the efforts. During this period, the children talk in abstract terms (except when pointing to the pictures); they co-operate by discussing each alternative, listening and replying to each other, making decisions and justifying their responses. They make no demands on their teacher during this time.

The task is then extended into a whole-class situation, with the teacher asking children to report back on the group decision. She is particularly pleased that children who do not often participate in whole-class discussions now do so, and she assumes that this is due to the security provided by the small group and the fact that all decisions are joint rather than individual.

The task set a problem (in the form of a decision to be made over alternatives) which must be resolved in order to fulfil the task demand. A similar task based on a family predicament (where can granny sleep when she comes to stay in an already crowded house: on the floor, in the bunks, on the settee, in the parents' bed, and so on?) leads to similar argument. Again there is a problem to be solved. The teacher states:

> 'I deliberately designed the tasks so that there was not an obvious solution for each problem. There was never an occasion when each group came to the same solution. This, I believe, shows that the problems were open-ended. It also meant that the class discussion after each session was broad and lively.'

The element of problem-solving does seem central to the development of groupwork tasks. Simply asking young children to discuss a topic, even if it is about something with which they are familiar or have a good deal of experience may not be useful. This was demonstrated when a group of infants was asked to discuss and then write about their mothers, in preparation for Mother's Day. Such a task does not incorporate a problem and the resulting talk is quite different in kind.

Suzanne

Martin

In a group, talk and write about your Mum. Help each other with the writing. End-product: individual writing about 'My Mum'

Katie

Stewart

Joyce

Although the children are quite willing to discuss their mothers, and do so at some length, their talk lacks direction and purpose and later descends to argument over whose mum is the best. The justifications they offer for the 'best mum' become competitive (eg, who gives most pocket money), rather than thoughtful.

'I just really like my mum, she's the best in the world.'
'No she's not. My mum's better than your mum. My mum's miles better than yours.'
'No. Your mum might be better than my mum to you but my mum's better than your mum to me.'

(b) Discussion of statements. The exact phrasing of a task becomes especially important in the context of problem-solving. For example, an English task asks pupils to discuss a series of statements about stories. A selection of these statements is given below.

- Stories are important to people.
- Stories should be shared and passed on.
- Stories are a waste of time because they aren't true.
- Parents should tell their children stories.
- The best stories are true stories.

However, the demand also is that pupils should 'decide which ones you agree with, which you disagree with, and those that you are not sure about. Be ready to give reasons for your decisions.' It is these decisions that are central and that encourage argument and justification; it is the need for decision-making that focuses the children's responses.

Katherine

Lizzie

> Four children discuss a series of statements about stories. End-product: sharing opinions with the class.

Nicky

Michelle

A group of nine-year-olds discuss the statements, and some short extracts of talk demonstrate the way in which they approach the task.

Nicky: Stories are important to people.
Lizzie: Well they could be if they are about themselves.

Michelle:	They learn more.
Katherine:	Yes they are.
Nicky:	Yeah. I think they are if they're true.
Lizzie:	Yes.
Katherine:	Also they could help people, a thing about them.
Nicky:	I know ... if they were about they ...
Katherine:	People enjoy stories.
Nicky:	Not all the time.
Lizzie:	Yes.
Michelle:	They get to know more ... what happens in life.
Nicky:	That's if it's a true story.
Lizzie:	I don't think you learn much from Sleeping Beauty.
Michelle:	Even if they're not true.
Katherine:	I think if they're not true stories, they might be make believe, but they can count.
Nicky:	You like reading them and get the idea of the story.

Later in the conversation, Lizzie pursues the idea of stories for 'learning', whereas Katherine, in particular, pursues the idea of stories for 'enjoyment'.

Katherine:	OK. Stories are a waste of time.
Lizzie:	Not really.
Michelle:	No, because you can enjoy a story.
Lizzie:	I mean if it was a story that went nowhere ... In the end ... it didn't teach you anything that would be a waste of time.
Michelle:	It's something to do.
Katherine:	Yes, but what if it's exciting and you really like it and you're interested in it? Something to do. Even if it doesn't sort of teach you anything, it's enjoyable.

It is not actually clear in the instructions to this task whether a group consensus is asked for, or merely for individuals to share their opinions with group members. What becomes apparent is that these children do have different opinions and, although their discussion is tentative, they are willing to pursue their ideas.

A group of three boys are involved in the same task.

Mark:	Parents should tell their children stories.
Tony:	No.
William:	Yes, yes.
Mark:	Yes because then they can learn how to read.

Tony: Only if they're little, but if they're old like us we've got to learn to read sometime.

William: Yeah but that's a different matter.

Peter: That's true Tony. Because we've got to learn to read sometime.

Tony: Cause they learn when they're little. Cause my sister, Sarah she can't learn and she's 12.

William: She's not little then.

Peter: You know.

Tony: Because my sister didn't really get enough reading. She had to go to Speech Therapy like me, but . . . and she can't really read really hard words.

Although these children deviate slightly from the task, it is interesting that these nine-year-olds clearly believe that reading is important, that story reading and telling relates to learning to read and that failure to read is due to a lack of reading when little – all reflecting the current wisdom!

(c) **Computer tasks.** Many computer tasks are commonly considered to be good examples of problem-solving activities: different responses to a program will lead to different outcomes, for better or worse, and the problem-solving is enshrined in the decision-making processes which need to be undertaken by children in order to make progress.

Two headteachers (one from a First and one from a Middle school) used a computer game to promote co-operative groupwork in their classrooms. Both believed that this would be an ideal problem-solving task:

'In my mind this simulation was the perfect work experience for children – it had everything! Adventure. The unknown. Co-operative decision-making. Extension of children's language. An end result in the form of a log-book written up after the simulation based on their experiences.'

But they both found that talk round the computer centred almost entirely on:

'what to do next in terms of functional procedures, for example, press the space bar and move to square C3. There was little of the expected language enrichment, little of the anticipated debate or verbal reasoning.'

The instructional talk was seldom in the form of a discussion of the problems to be overcome; more often it was simply ideas being floated:

David: What happens when we get to the middle? Are we going
          to go down?
Rachel: Yeah, we're going down.
Nick: OK. N7.

Children make decisions about what to do next, but they do not seem
to discuss reasons for their choice. They also seem to work as much
by trial and error as by judgement, and one-word answers are often
adequate.

Nick: What about W3?
David: Alright.
          [Nick types, David reads: Open sea, keep on sailing.]
Nick: Go on a diagonal way.
David: Go across next.
Nick: Across.
David: Yeah.
Rachel: Straight across.

The computer dominates the interaction in that the children respond
to it. At the same time, it reinforces casual testing out of possibilities
without any need to think through a reasoned hypothesis, for this
proves to be a perfectly adequate way to make progress. The computer
programme certainly does not ask children to justify choices or to
discuss their decision-making. Later, when the same children work co-
operatively on a log book about their computer adventure, their
teachers report that the task was of better quality.

It might be argued that children are effective problem-solvers if they
readily work their way through a computer programme by means of
trial and error. Yet this surely cannot be the intention of programme
designers who emphasise the importance of the development of logic
and problem-solving through language?

Interestingly, the two headteachers found, in a survey of local
teachers, that '98% felt that a computer simulation would be an
enriching language experience; 95% felt that hands on experience
would also develop the quality of children's language.' Certainly this
had been their own assumption, encouraged by the fact that: 'These
programs often have gloriously detailed glossy packaging, contain an
impressive document full of the technical and educational benefits, and
more recently even include attainment targets for the National
Curriculum.'

However, they now sound a warning about assumptions. Some
computer programs may encourage more recognition of problems than

others, but at present we have no research on this. We can only suggest that however useful, exciting or motivating any individual program is, teachers should not automatically assume that it will encourage children to dwell on problems and to talk them through in a logical or speculative manner, rather than to complete the program as quickly as possible. In the long-term it might be possible to train children to be more aware of problems, more critical of each other's decision-making, and to question and challenge instead of agreeing without discussion. Teacher intervention could be planned to encourage children to talk in different ways. Yet there might be little incentive for pupils to elaborate if this activity did not actually help them to advance through the computer programme. However, in terms of management, computer work can be important in that it frees the teacher from a group, and especially since it tends to hold children's attention firmly on-task for extended periods of time; it is also useful in the practice it gives in terms of small-group co-operation.

(d) **Prediction of circumstances.** One of the potential benefits of a computer task is that it could allow children to speculate about consequences of actions and plan accordingly. However, this does not occur if they choose to work by trial and error and if this method is reinforced by being proved successful. Yet even children in a reception class demonstrate that they are able to predict circumstances by projecting themselves into an imaginary, though realistic, situation.

Four children have been given two life-size rag dolls – a boy doll and a girl doll known as Polly and Billy. Their task was to dress one of the dolls appropriately for a weekend stay with grandmother at the seaside, and to pack a suitcase. The teacher says that she 'wanted to provide a "talk" task which was also a "problem-solving" task.'

Caroline

Jenny	Four children dress a life-size rag doll and pack a suitcase for a trip to grandmother. End-product: a dressed doll and a packed suitcase.	Lisa

Elaine

The children immediately tackle the task seriously, with a mixture of both talk relating to action and the immediate context – picking up, examining and choosing appropriate objects – and talk that is entirely in the abstract – predicting a future possibility, relating it to their own past experiences, justifying their choices, and so on. Other children from the same class who tackle the activity at different times respond in similar ways. Some examples are given below.

Caroline: As she's going on a long journey she could . . . as it's going to be pitch black when she gets there . . . she could . . . put her nightie on and her slippers on and travel there.

Lisa: Maybe she could wear these and be dressed for going to the beach and then . . .

Jenny: Yes.

Lisa: And then when she sees Nannie she could put her dressing gown on afterwards when she wants to go to sleep.

Elaine: Boots, boots.

Caroline: Just in case it gets cold.

Lisa: And some boots in case it goes raining.

Interestingly, throughout the task, Elaine is a major provider of ideas for what to wear and pack and it is the other children who justify her choices.

Richard: She'll need her slippers. She'll need her shoes. Aha, a clean pair in case the others get dirty.

Michael: Ah yes.

Michael: . . . She needs to wear boots in case she goes in mud.

Richard: She'll need a towel.

Michael: In case she needs a shower or a bath, in case she goes into the water.

Richard: In case she goes into the sea.

Richard: I don't think she'll need any jumpers.

Patrick: It'll be boiling hot.

In the extract below, Joe and Timothy seem, in particular, simply to be enjoying their own language.

Timothy: And he'll have to have a toothbrush.

Joe: Yes.

Rosemary: To clean his teeth.

Joe: Or they'll get bad and then be false.

Timothy: He won't need plimsoles.

Joe: No; cos he's not going plimsoling! We need them for the beach.

Timothy: He won't need his school tie 'cos he's not going tie-ering!

Joe: But he needs his jogging shoes on. He's going jogging.

The problem-solving encouraged by this task operates at different levels. For example, they do not find packing easy but all seem determined to make a good job of it:

Lisa: He'll need one of these tops just in case he gets cold.
John: Don't just dump them in!
Gareth: Fold them! This is good folding!
John: I'm trying to get this longer.
Lisa: Shall I help you?
John: Yes, you can try to get that longer.

There is discussion on which items are appropriate to fold into a suitcase, endless prediction of the kind of weather at the seaside, and awareness of the needs of a car journey.

Jason: You don't fold coats up.
Nigel: You do fold them up to go and stay with someone.
Jason: You don't. You wear them in case it's cold and you go when it's dark.

As might be predicted with reception children, the situation becomes 'real' for them and at times the doll is spoken to as a person:

Claire: It's only Polly invited, and Polly . . . you'd better behave yourself.
Lucy: Yes.
Claire: If you don't I'll just to take you straight home – back in the car.
Thomas: Polly you'd better get dressed otherwise you won't be able to go to your Nannie's will you? Come on, come on Polly. You're never like this are you?

Only one child actually comes to question the reality:

Phillip: Is the Nannie real or is she only pretend?
Jacob: It's real, real, real. I wonder how many nights he's staying.

(e) **The context of problem-solving.** The term 'problem-solving' needs to be given meaning in particular contexts. It is often characterised in terms of a task which has no 'correct' solution (thereby allowing for a wide range of contributions and ideas). For discussion activities this seems a reasonable assumption, as well as for certain kinds of construction task – for example, a bridge-building task – where there is no single 'best' or 'right' way to achieve the demand. Most of the tasks described in this section have allowed for this kind of wide-ranging discussion.

However, tasks which demand 'right' answers may also promote problem-solving. Several of the tasks chosen by teachers in our study demand an end-product to satisfy fairly precise requirements of 'correctness' – for example, making perfect three-dimensional shapes and drawing correct nets of these shapes. Such a task can be an excellent problem-solving activity if the ways and means of achieving the end-product are given to the children. Therein lies the problem – *how* to achieve their goal.

Tight and loose frameworks

Barnes and Todd (1977), in their detailed research study of lower secondary children, noticed that the co-operating teachers distinguished between 'loose' and 'tight' tasks for groupwork. Their descriptions and examples are particularly useful in terms of task design and their principles translate readily to the primary school context. Their distinction tends to reflect the difference between those activities that have 'correct' solutions and those that do not. Tight tasks are likely to need responses that are highly focussed; loose tasks are unlikely to need 'right' answers and responses can be more wide-ranging.

> '... teachers chose to set loose tasks when their pupils had much everyday knowledge that was relevant, as in "The Pearl" [the novel by Steinbeck] and in social studies topics such as "Gang Violence". They tended to set tighter topics in science, where the explanations they wanted were more removed from everyday ways of looking at things.'

It became clear that the extent to which tasks were 'tight' or 'loose' had a marked impact on ways of working and many problems emerged when teachers misjudged this impact. Barnes and Todd explain:

> 'There are considerable dangers ... in setting up too tight a series of directions. For example, in the "Bird's Eggs" task the initial instructions called for action and observation:

Crack the egg into a dish, without breaking the yolk.
Find a small white speck on the yolk.
What do you think this is?

This question was not, however, open to discussion solely on the basis of observation and the common-sense knowledge available to the children. Several of the groups did not find it easy to change their strategy from descriptive observation to the generating of a sequence of possible explanations of the white spot. (It is possible that there we have a clash between what the children thought of as normal learning strategies in school and the demands of this task.)

After our work with these groups we concluded that there is much to be said for ending even the tightest task with an open invitation to discuss other related issues which occur to pupils. Even the most experienced teacher cannot predict all the problems that face each group of his pupils in understanding the topic under discussion; he may have the responsibility for making available to pupils traditional ways of solving problems in that subject, but he should not forget their private problems of understanding which they may need to sort out first.'

This kind of task, though asking for hypothesis, actually has a 'correct' answer and is very different in nature from an example they give of a 'loose' task.

'In the introduction to "The Pearl", John Steinbeck says that the story may be a parable and that, "perhaps everyone takes his own meaning from it." Discuss among yourselves what you have found in the story so far – the "good and bad things, and black and white things and good and evil things," as Steinbeck says; and any points about the characters, the setting, the way the book is written, that you feel worth discussion. In spite of the length of these instructions they offer little constraint, explicit or implicit, to the replies. Moral issues from the story are to be discussed, but characters, setting and style are also relevant. Moreover, "everyone takes his own meaning from it" is an invitation to the pupils to regard their own sense of relevance of paramount. One could not have a much looser task than this.'

In this instance the 'loose' task allowed pupils to participate more easily than the 'tight' task, for they could use a wide range of personal experience to interpret the question.

Kerry (1983) provided some ideas on the different forms that discussion can take (Table 4.1). These are useful in enabling teachers to plan the purposes of specific discussion activities, although, in fact, it may not be possible to isolate each of these proposed features. So, for example, when looking for meaning in *The Pearl*, discussion could

Table 4.1

Discussion leading to a group action, eg planning a practical task	Discussion to clarify issues in a controversial field	Discussion to help build pupils' confidence	Discussion to make a decision, eg to adopt or reject a club rule	Discussion aimed at helping pupils to argue more effectively	Sharing information or experience, eg after an outing

touch on controversial issues; such issues might lead to argument; progress might be dependent on sharing ideas and experiences; and each (or all) of these might be an objective of the teacher in setting the task.

Eggins *et al.* (for the School's Council, 1979), however, advocate 'tight' tasks, arguing particularly that in the early stages of groupwork a narrow focus will give a sense of security to those who are unused to talking and to the low attaining child. Ideally, they suggest 'the form of instructions or questions should offer the children a secure framework but should not be so restrictive that any form of exploratory thinking is curtailed.' So, for example, in the earliest stages of groupwork, an exercise such as a Cloze Procedure comprehension task will encourage talk within close limits; this experience can then be used to broaden out into more general discussion tasks.

Biott (1984) also suggests from his own collaborative efforts with teachers that it is most appropriate to start co-operative groupwork with simple, brief activities with a narrow focus before attempting more generalised problem-solving activities. In particular, he recommends the use of production tasks as a starting point: 'problem-solving activities which have tangible materials that are handled and which have a specific outcome have been found very useful.' Such a task might take a form such as: 'Design a bridge using the materials provided. When finished, it must be strong enough to hold a Matchbox car.'

Biott suggests that when problems inherent in co-operative work have been worked through at the 'production' level, and tasks have been carefully evaluated by the teacher and the group, pupils may be better prepared for 'looser', more abstract discussion. In this context it must also be appropriate to consider the ages of the children involved. Our own research shows that where co-operative discussion is prevalent, when pupils become used to, and well-practised in, this way of working, and when the 'problem' is understood, then even young children may be able to cope with a wide range of discussion activities. However, there are also occasions when children at the top of the primary school continue to struggle with more open-ended discussion, especially when the problem set is too hard and the pupils' background knowledge or experience is lacking.

Planning

One way of focussing pupils' ideas for working on a problem-solving task is through the medium of planning. Pupil-planning can be considered particularly important in the context of groupwork when joint planning will be necessary. Yet in their recent science report, for example, HMI (1989c) argue that 'much promising work falters because children are not taught well enough how to plan investigations.' Planning can be formally built into an activity with the teacher making it clear that a planning stage is essential before moving into action; or it can be observed throughout a task.

The extracts of talk below demonstrate how different groups of children are either aware, or unaware, of a need to plan and there is some evidence that interesting variations may occur according to the composition of the group.

Some six-year-old children have been given half-an-hour to build a Robinson Crusoe shelter out of Quadro (a large scale set of construction materials). There are three groups – one is all boys, one all girls and one mixed.

The boys make no attempt at planning. They move straight into the action:

James:	You start on the roof Tom.
Tom:	I'll need that bit up there.
James:	Now turn it upside down . . .
Tony:	That's gonna be the roof is it? Quite good.
Tom:	Yes quite . . . I've never done this before.
Andrew:	That goes there. Ah!
Tony:	Now, do I, what do we do next?
James:	We need one of these bits, but . . . one of them.
Tony:	A straight bit, do we need a straight bit?
James:	Yes we do, like that bit here, to make it go down.
Tony:	Tom, we need a straight bit, to make it go straight, you get it.
Tom:	Here you are.
James:	Now we're stuck, aren't we?

The girls, however, do plan by imagining shapes in the abstract:

Lucy: How shall we start then?
Anne: We'll make a ladder going up.
Jane: We'll make a square first.
Anne: Make a square first, then make a ladder, climb up so it goes over the top and then you can climb both ways. OK?
Susan: How about doing the ladder both sides.
Jane: Front and back?
Anne: Put a ladder going down and a window.
Lucy: We'll put the window there [pointing in the air]. Well, somewhere.
Lucy: We mustn't forget to do the roof.
Anne: Shall we start then?
Lucy: I'll start here [picks up a tube].
Jane: This fits in here, right?
Anne: OK.

The mixed group seem to discuss and plan as they use the materials together:

Elizabeth: What are we going to do then?
John: It has to be big enough for one person. We'll need these bits.
David: We definitely need these bits. This we definitely need (tubes).
Lisa: But David, what about these? [connectors]
David: Pass me one Lisa.
Lisa: You need two [gives two].
John: Liz, that won't work, you should try that one instead.
Elizabeth: Alright, clever.
Elizabeth: How big, how big will it be?
John: Big enough for one person.
Lisa: Yeah, one of us.
John: No David, you've got the wrong one, look, [shows right connector] you want one with two.
David: Oh yeah. Where, where, where, there.
John: Here David, I'll help.

If we compare the first line of talk from each group, we can compare approaches.

Boys: 'You start on the roof Tom' – which allows for no planning.
Girls: 'How shall we start then?' – which is far more tentative and therefore invites planning.

Mixed: 'What are we going to do then?' – which also invites planning, is spoken by a girl [Elizabeth] and receives a response by a boy, but does not lead to prolonged discussion.

Interestingly, Elizabeth continues to question and challenge throughout the activity, as if she really did feel the need to have planned in advance. The responses to her questions must have been unsatisfactory!

Elizabeth: John, I'd like to know what you're doing [ignored] . . . What are you doing that for?
Lisa: 'Cos we are . . . the corners.
Elizabeth: Why?
John: We need a pole across there.

When the teacher questions these children about their planning, only the all girls group has positive answers, for example:

Teacher: Do you think you shared your ideas with each other?
Jane: We sat and talked to each other at the beginning and we all knew what we were doing.
Teacher: Who do you think had the best ideas in your group?
Jane: All of us.
Teacher: Did you share your ideas?
Lucy: A little bit. We talked a bit before we started.
Teacher: Did that help you make the house?
Lucy: It did really, we all knew what we're all doing and didn't get it all wrong.

These examples suggest that the boys may find it more difficult to plan than girls, indeed not even seeing a place for it. We could not generalise from this one classroom, but there is a further evidence of boys finding planning hard.

For example, a group of seven-year-olds have been asked by the teacher to draw an electric circuit diagram, but to discuss first how to plan it out. Thus a planning stage has deliberately been built into the task.

Anthony: Have you done your discussion?
Ben: She (the teacher) said do your pictures.
Anthony: After you've done your discussion.
Ben: Have you got any ideas . . .?
    (30 seconds later)

Andrew: Let's draw a battery.
Ben: We've got to discuss first.
Andrew: Yes we've got to . . .
Ben: Have you got any ideas?

No discussion takes place at this point. It is clear these boys not know what it is they can discuss. It seems likely that the teacher has set up a situation that is too artificial for them, especially if it is indeed the case that boys find planning hard anyway. Ben really does try to follow the teacher's request, but he fails to plan in the abstract; instead he talks through what he is doing as he attaches the clips to the circuit:

Ben: We've got to discuss first and then we're going to do it. So then we clip this on like that and clip this on like that.

It seems from these examples that teachers should not make assumptions about their pupils' abilities to plan; as HMI suggest, it may be a skill which needs to be taught. This is illustrated by the following example of a response to a task which the teacher expects will incorporate a significant planning stage. Some children at the top of middle school are asked to plan and make a table game. This kind of activity is not new to them; although materials have been laid out by the teacher, the design stage is expected to be an abstract activity. However, one group immediately turns to the materials and their talk focusses on these. They clearly decide instantly to make a snooker-type game.

Graham: We've got the . . . what's it called?
Chris: Yeah.
Graham: Cushions?
Amanda: It's the cushions, right?
Chris: To go up the side.
Graham: In the middle of the cushion on . . .
Janice: Yeah, we've got the . . . Chris found these rods that we can use.
Graham: Yes, if we choose.
Janice: Yeah, if we choose they're both the same length and they really are long enough. Here's a demonstration.
Chris: You've got one cue.
Janice: And it went through the bridge.
Graham: When it goes through the bridge, it falls down the hole?
Janice: Falls in the pocket.
Graham: Then you just take it out and put it on the side?

Amanda: No, it goes, it just goes through the bridge and that's the goal.

Turning directly to the materials may be a realistic way of approaching this task, and there is certainly some argument about the form the game should take. Yet, if a teacher is concerned about the development of abstract planning, then in this instance it has been unsuccessful. Other children from the same class, however, respond to the same task demand in different ways. Contrary to the findings with younger children, it is now a group of boys, led by Graham, who enter into a discussion at an abstract planning level:

Graham: Listen everybody. Quiet. Do you have an idea? Do you have an idea, do you have an idea to start with . . .?
Darren: I reckon it should be a pin ball machine or a marble maze.
Peter: I think we should do a pin ball machine.
Graham: I reckon, right, we could mix them all together. A pin ball machine and a bit of a maze with a little bit of levers so that they go with a ball so that the marbles go into the little buckets.
All: Yeah, that's a good idea.
Graham: See, I'm brilliant.
Richard: Yes you are.
David: Right, let's draw it down, get a pencil.

What is not clear is why some children work in this more abstract way while others do not, and whether this relates to pupil ability, gender, age or previous experience; nor in this instance is it clear whether the end-product was better because of this kind of planning. Further research in this area is necessary before any valid conclusions can be reached. If, however, teachers value abstract thought and are concerned to promote it, it seems that a planning demand as the first stage of an action-related task could be an appropriate method for its development.

Summary

To summarise this chapter on the cognitive demands of tasks, there are several features of task design which are central and will have a clear impact on the ways on which children work:

(a)   the form of the task (that is, whether it is a 'production' or a 'discussion' activity) is clearly a major distinction and dominates the task design and the pupil's response; underlying this distinction is the suggestion that groupwork is dependent on problem-solving activity.

(b)   the extent to which an activity contains a problem-solving element and the way this is set up so that children recognise the problem, whether or not there is a 'correct' end-product, and what 'decisions' need to be taken.

(c)   the framework of the task, which can be conceived in terms of 'looseness' or 'tightness'; that is, the extent to which possibilities are widened or narrowed by the task content and instructions.

(d)   whether or not a pupil-planning stage is required as a prerequisite to further activity.

The teachers' choices of task content are apparent in every example that we present here and throughout the book. We do not otherwise take it on ourselves to recommend specific tasks, but anticipate that our discussions will constantly provide a framework for task design. Having considered in some detail the cognitive demand of tasks, it is now appropriate to turn to the social demand. The social demand offers a further dimension to task design but, as outlined earlier, it always remains closely linked to the cognitive requirements of an activity, as the tasks described in the following chapter clearly demonstrate.

5 Designing tasks: Social aspects

The social demand of the task

Throughout the previous chapter, we have shown how the cognitive demand of the task dominates the ways in which children tackle their work and has a great deal of influence on the ways in which children talk. Our own research has highlighted how the abstract/action dichotomy relates to the content in terms of discussion and production tasks; other research suggests that task content in terms of 'tightness' or 'looseness' of the demand is central to the way in which the activity is pursued, and so on. However, the social demand – as represented in our three models for co-operative tasks – also has a bearing on talk and approaches to the work, since it relates to the kinds of co-operative endeavour that are demanded.

First, the three models are summarised:

1 Children work individually on identical tasks for individual products, but are asked to talk to each other about their work, to help each other, thereby establishing co-operative endeavour.
2 Children work individually on 'jigsaw' elements of a task, so that a certain amount of co-operation is built into the task, especially in terms of planning and organisation.
3 Children work jointly on one task for a joint outcome, so that co-operation is of paramount importance.

These three models demonstrate that groupwork is not enshrined within one single, specific form of classroom management, but encompasses different approaches with children working in different ways. In addition, each of the models will have a different impact on the ways in which children work and talk.

In order to illustrate these features of groupwork, a series of lessons are presented below in which pupils are working on practical activities for either maths or technology or are focussing on language tasks. Each model for groupwork is considered in turn, and it is hoped that the examples and discussion will enable the reader to understand more fully the relationship between the choice of task and the children's response to it.

1(a)   Working individually on identical tasks for individual products: Maths

In the first task shown below, four children are making cuboids from card for a maths activity. The group of seven- and eight-year-olds has been asked to co-operate as the extracts of talk below will show. Although each child is working individually, the context of the group is considered to be important. The conversation is slightly difficult to follow since the children are all reporting their own progress to the others.

Peter

Tania

| Each child is making a cuboid from card. End-product: four cuboids |

Richard

Susan

Teacher:	Remember you're working as a group, not on your own. Help each other.
Peter:	Oh, cooey, I've done it wrong.
Richard:	Brill, finished. Do you think that's a perfect . . .?
Tania:	I'm going to make another one because I did that one wrong. It won't stick up like that. Something's wrong there.
Susan:	Oh, I have to do this again, it's rubbish. Tania, I have to do this again 'cos it's rubbish, isn't it?
Peter:	I've finished nearly – ha, ha.
Teacher:	Well you must ask the rest of your group, because you might not have done. I didn't hear you asking anyone.
Richard:	I asked Tania – the nearest.

It can be seen here that, although the task itself does not demand co-operation, the teacher wants the children to work together, to help each other, to be aware of what others are doing and how they are working. The group (rather than the individual) is given responsibility for the quality of each end product and the pupils need, therefore, to turn to each other to check for correctness. Although the teacher controls this process at the beginning of the lesson, she quickly moves away and the children clearly show immediate concern for one another and the quality of the work.

Tania: It doesn't matter, just fold it again right. It doesn't matter, it doesn't matter . . . you don't have to start again.
Susan: I gotta do it again.
Peter: There is something wrong with it.
Tania: Let's make sure, where's yours?
Susan: There's something wrong with it.
Richard: Yeah there is . . . there must be.
Richard: Brill . . . it's getting more and more good.
Susan: Is that correct Tania?
Tania: Mmmmm . . . Yep.

This type of group response is not unusual; when asked to co-operate by the teacher, and when this is reinforced, children across the primary age-range are willing and able to work in a similar way, helping and taking an interest in each other's work. That they are working on their own individual end-products does not prevent a high level of co-operation, if demanded.

1(b) Working individually on identical tasks for individual products: English

Mary Anne

Neil
Each child is drawing a poster to illustrate a poem which they have read together. End-product: four posters
      Samantha

Matthew

An example of an individual language activity is seen when a group of nine- and ten-year-olds are given a long poem, *The Forest of Tangle*, which is read both with the teacher and by the group. The children are then asked to draw individual posters to illustrate the poem and told also that they may be challenged about its meaning. Each drawing needs to reflect the description and sense of the poem, and the children thus search for meaning as this becomes important to their illustration. The activity of 'meaning-making' is apparent within the children's talk as they describe and discuss their work.

Samantha:	Tangle . . . you could draw the man in a tangle with two trees.
Mary Anne:	No I'm not. I'm sitting him down with his hands over his face crying. He's an old man isn't he?
Samantha:	I dunno. Yes I think . . . Does it say old? Does it say man?
Mary Anne:	An old . . . yeah . . . It says 'the old King of the Makers'.
Samantha:	If it says 'King' it must be a man.

The precise meaning of individual words also becomes important to the process of understanding.

Mary Anne:	What does faggot mean?
Samantha:	Faggot?
Mary Anne:	Yeah.
Samantha:	What it is, is this sheep's heart they eat in Scotland.
Neil:	Bevy, do you know what bevy means?
Mary Anne:	Faggot does it say? Oh, that's not a faggot . . . faggot's like a meatball, I reckon. Or it might be a sheep's heart.
Neil:	Mary Anne. Do you know what bevy is? Do you know what bevy is?
Mary Anne:	Bevy. I think it means a man who's not getting any bills because no-one's coming to buy his things. [She is attempting to piece together information to make sense of the word.]

Neil is not convinced by this (incorrect) answer and later asks the teacher for a definition which he reports back to the group. However, Mary Anne's attempt to make sense of the words is important; that she is wrong would only become problematic if the rest of the group ridiculed her when Neil provided a different meaning. In fact, the children listened to the given definition, 'a lot of', and tried to work it into the text.

In another language task, where the object of the lesson is a piece of writing from each individual child, similar kinds of discussion take place.

Sophie   Holly

Four children discuss a story they have read to themselves. End-product: individual written opinions on the story.

Luke

Neil

Four children aged eleven are asked to read a story to themselves and then write their opinions and comments on it, especially why they like or dislike it. However, alongside their personal account, they are also encouraged to talk about the story, to share their ideas and to discuss their opinions. An extract of this discussion is given below:

Sophie: The ending was hopeless.
Holly: Was it? Do you think it was?
Luke: I liked the ending.
Sophie: It was too soppy though.
Luke: Too soppy?
Neil: Well I like it when they die at endings. It makes a lot more funnier. It's a lot more good.
Holly: Well that's very nice isn't it? [sarcastically]
Neil: It's a lot more good – like – like – if I wrote a story I'd go 'as he swings his head with his sword' and stop the book there and they'd want to buy the next book wouldn't they?
Holly: No, probably wouldn't – because not many people like animals being killed.
Neil: They would.

The four children clearly find the story worthy of their consideration. They demonstrate an understanding of the story genre (though the preferences for endings may reflect a gender bias); they are prepared to challenge each other's ideas and justify their opinions. They are also keen to report to other group members what they have written and seem to anticipate comment or criticism.

Interestingly, they do not copy each other's work – each piece of writing is different – but the discussion does seem to spark off ideas. They also check other pupils' work for spelling and punctuation mistakes.

Although it is not possible to ascertain the extent to which the group context has an impact on their completed pieces of writing, the reasoned sharing of ideas must be an important aspect of their personal development. For this task, as for the poster-drawing task, the demand to co-operate as a group, to discuss and look for meaning together, does not seem to pose difficulties for the children and certainly does not detract from their individual end-products.

2 *Working individually on 'Jigsaw' elements for a joint outcome: Maths*

James

Paul

> Each child is making a different-sized box from a piece of squared paper, 10 cm × 10 cm. End-product: as many boxes as can be made from the same-sized paper.

Natalie

Lucy

Four six-year-old children are working on the same maths task in a mixed ability group. They have been shown, and have practised, one example of a specific method for making an open-topped box using squared paper measuring ten by ten centimetres. As they have now been asked to work as a group to find out how many different boxes can be made from that same-sized piece of paper, they *must* operate co-operatively to establish the different possibilities, and to decide who is doing what. Since they are not yet able to work out theoretically how many boxes can be made from this sized paper, they now test this out by practical means.

The diagrams in Figure 5.1 illustrate how the children are expected to make their boxes. They also demonstrate the consequences of cutting away different-sized corners. The children start making a box each, constantly reporting on their own activity. It is important that each pupil makes a box of a different size in order to fulfil the task demand.

James: Do you just go up to 2? [James is asking Natalie how to count the squares to cut out for the corners.]

Natalie: One, two, one, two, one, two [demonstrates where to cut].

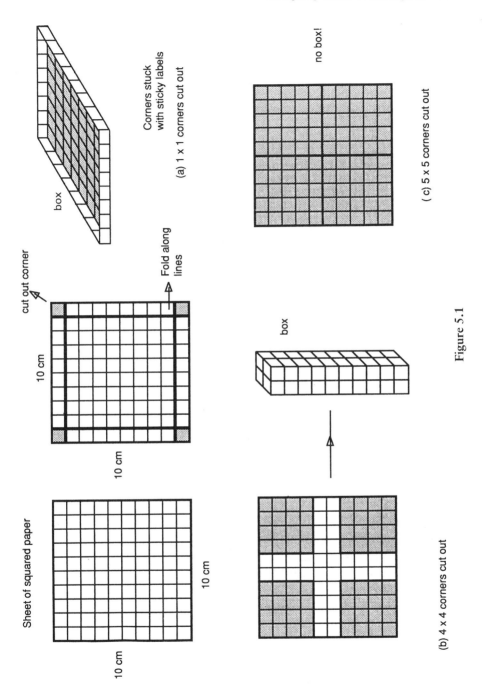

Figure 5.1

James:	I'm doing a 4 by 4 [ie, 4 by 4 squares cut from each corner].
Paul:	I'm doing 11 by 11 [the group laughs, presumably since they are aware that this is impossible].
Lucy:	I'm doing 3 by 3.
James:	I'm doing 4 by 4.
Paul:	I'm cutting out one square from each corner.
Natalie:	One square?
Paul:	Yeah [laughs].
	[There is now a period wherein they can all be heard counting to themselves.]
Lucy:	I'm doing a 3 by 3 which leaves 4 in the middle.
James:	Mine only leaves 2 in the middle.
Lucy:	Two in the middle?
James:	Yeah [laughs] Look!
Lucy:	5 by 5
James:	[laughs] That's not going to get anywhere!
James /Lucy:	[counting together] 1,2,3,4,5; 1,2,3,4,5; 1,2,3,4,5; 1, 2,3,4,5.
Natalie:	That's a 10 by 10 now ... I mean ... [James cuts, counting as he goes].
James:	I think she won't be able to make one out of 5 by 5 [group laughter]. [James holds up a 5 by 5 square to show his 10 by 10 square is now cut into four separate pieces.] You can make one out of 4 by 4 but you can't make one out of 5 by 5.

Video-tape of this incident shows that the children are totally involved and really excited by James' discovery. Since he is demonstrating and talking to the group, his prediction that 5 by 5 will not work is not only proven to the others, but seems also to be fully understood by them.

The children soon decide that there are only four different boxes that can be made from their paper. These boxes are carefully finished and presented as the group's end-product. (James, however, later realised that any number of different-sized boxes could be made if he took account of $\frac{1}{2}$ squares and even smaller denominations!)

It can be seen from this description that the children work in similar ways to those in the lesson described for model 1. However, although each pupil is working on a box, it is important that each box is different. The end-products are similar, but not identical. Only by making different boxes, with different numbers of squares cut away, will they be able to work out how many boxes can be made from the same-sized piece of paper. When an individual completes his own box, the task demand is not necessarily fulfilled; decisions have to be made by the group as to when they have all done what is required.

3 (a)   *Working jointly on one task for a joint outcome: English*

Working co-operatively as a whole group is not always easy, especially when the topic for discussion is difficult. A group of five pupils are asked to read two accounts of the same story. The first version is a transcript of the spoken story; the second is a written version. The children are expected to comment on differences between the two in terms of quality, interest, style, and so on, and then produce a group report.

Lesley

Joanne	A group discussion on the differences between a spoken and written story. End-product: a group report
Timothy	

Rosie   Darren

Several group members make a real effort to tackle this task, both at the cognitive level and at the social level, taking heed of the request to provide a group report. Their talk illustrates the kinds of difficulty they encountered with this.

Lesley: We all prefer the written version.
Rosie: What are you writing down now?
Darren: I haven't done it yet.
Rosie: We all preferred the written version.
Darren: Pardon?
Timothy: I didn't.
Rosie: Well, nearly all of us preferred the written version then.
Lesley: No, because there's only five of us.
Rosie: OK, four of us liked the written version.

They continue to have the same kinds of problem throughout the lesson and clearly become very annoyed with each other on occasion:

Lesley: Well, I'm not doing anything.
Joanne: I know you're not. That's the problem, Lesley.
Rosie: Somebody have some good ideas.

As a group, they seem frustrated by not really being able to do the task that has been set. The following extract of discussion shows that the children are 'stuck' at the level of 'primitive argument', unable to explain to others why they feel as they do, and unwilling to come to agreement.

Rosie:	OK. What have you written now?
Lesley:	The spoken version was boring but no-one else seems to think so.
Joanne:	No-one else thinks so.
Rosie:	Oh I suppose not.
Lesley:	Well say: 'Most of us think the spoken version . . .'
Joanne:	I don't think it was boring. I don't think boring. It was different.
Rosie:	I think it was different.
Lesley:	I think . . .
Joanne:	It was different, but it wasn't boring.
Timothy:	It wasn't boring.
Lesley:	I think it was boring and not different.
Rosie:	Darren, you haven't said much towards it.
Lesley:	Yes Darren, what do you think?
Darren:	Darren has what . . .?

It seems likely that it is the difficulty with the task itself that upsets the social relationships within the group, since on other occasions they do not aggravate each other in the same way.

3 (b) *Working jointly on one task for a joint outcome: Technology*

When a task demands only one artefact to be produced by the whole group, co-operation is essential, but not always easily achieved, especially when the children are unused to working in this way.

	David	Jane	
Paul	Four children are building a small cart together. End-product: one cart		Stacey

For this technology task, the four group members (eight-year-olds) are really sharing activities. They do not all participate either in talk or action all the time, but observation of the task made it clear that each child was involved throughout, that they listened to each other's discussion and decision-making, that they watched each other, and that the end-product was truly a group effort. In Cowie and Ruddock's terms, this is a typical group 'production task'.

Jane and David are making the axles for their cart; they work out the necessary measurements together, gently arguing, but both seeking understanding of what they are doing.

Jane: Here it is, measure across the box to see how long the axle should be and remember to add on 2 centimetres on each end so you have enough room to fit on the wheels.
David: Wait a minute, I'm doing the thing, I need to mark . . .
Jane: You need to leave . . .
David: Twenty centimetres.
Jane: It doesn't have to be, no, 'cos see how long.
David: Twenty centimetres, it . . .
Jane: Look across here.
David: It needs to be four more centimetres.
Jane: You need to leave off 2 centimetres.
David: No you don't.
Jane: Measure across the box to see how long the axle should be. Remember to add on two centimetres on each end.
David: Add on, not take away.
Jane: Yes.
David: So it needs to be eighteen centimetres.
Jane: Why?
David: Because it has to . . . look that is 16 cm, 17, 18 add on 2 . . . 18 centimetres.
Jane: No 18 add 2 . . . 20.
David: Yes.

Three children then become involved together, making full use of each other:

Jane: Can you push that down, Stacey? Push that down, keep hold of that, push it, now push that.
David: Now make two little ones . . . wait a minute, here you are, no I think that's too big. No it isn't. There you are, there's another . . . don't matter, don't matter if they're too small 'cos it don't matter.
Jane: Got the other, make sure you're careful because it's got the white glue on.

Unfortunately, Paul does not find it so easy to participate in the group.

His attempt to join in – 'I don't know what to do' – is fairly negative, and yet he is interested in the task and clearly wants to be involved. When he is not heeded by the others, he rephrases his question and demonstrates his enthusiasm.

>   Paul: What can I do? I've got the sticking bit
>   . . . I've got the wood sticking, I've got this one . . . no I've got this one . . . what shall I stick? . . . one of those and a pencil?

Unfortunately, Paul is rebuffed.

>   Jane: Sorry, Paul, Stacey's doing it. Put it on this one for her. Because you're not my best friend, wait a minute. There's plenty of sawing, look these and these.

Gradually he gains responses, for example:

>   Paul: I'm not doing anything . . . What shall I do?
>   Stacey: See if you can hold it there.

Jane then organises the situation to give each group member a chance to saw.

>   Jane: Paul and Stacey can do the next bit of sawing.

These extracts show yet again the way in which talk relates to the actions necessary to complete the task. David at one point attempts an explanation of how to calculate the length of the axles, but this never actually reaches an abstract level, since he turns to the materials to demonstrate his point.

In terms of co-operation, the joint nature of the task created a few difficulties with regard to participation, yet during a short period of time, these pupils seem to make progress in their personal relationships and, despite their young age, are co-operating effectively to complete their group cart. Although friendship patterns clearly have an impact on the group interaction and Paul at first appears to be somewhat of an outsider, his own persistence and Jane's powers of organisation enable him to be drawn into the group. Indeed Jane shows evidence of an almost instant change of heart, from rebuffing Paul – 'you're not my best friend', to 'wait a minute. There's plenty of sawing . . .', thus accepting Paul as a useful group member.

What happens when the demand for co-operation is changed: A comparison of two lessons

We have just considered a lesson in which David, Jane, Stacey and Paul are making a cart together. We now consider this task in more detail, as well as a second lesson in which the same children are making individual carts. These two lessons not only allow an understanding of the context in which the group activities were set up and how the teacher planned them, but also allow for a comparison of lessons where the children are the same, the task is the same, but where the task structure, and hence the co-operative demand, is changed.

These sessions represent a complete change in practice for the teacher – from ability and friendship groups and an integrated day, to mixed ability co-operative groups with the whole class working on the same task at the same time. They are of particular interest in their design since in the first lesson the children will work together in order to rehearse and practise cart-building skills. In the second lesson, the teacher hopes that these skills can be transferred to the building of individual models.

The Group: A mixed ability, heterogenous group of eight-year-olds. The whole class has been divided into similar groups and they all work on the same task at the same time.

The task: The teacher has planned a series of lessons on building 'carts'; her notes are reproduced below and give a good idea of how a model-building project developed over several weeks. (The sessions refer to those lessons at which a researcher was present.)

Session 1: *'This is the third in a series of "lessons" – the group have already produced "free" models and "improved" models and are now tackling a set model. The children will use my written illustrations and diagrams. The children are working as a group to produce one model only – so demanding group co-operation. For this day only, I shall provide glue from a glue gun which will demand extra help from me. Usually the children will use slow-setting glue.*

Session 2: *The task is similar to the previous work. However, this time each child is working on his/her individual model. They are at varying stages – all the children have chosen and covered boxes to make a particular wheeled vehicle. They have all measured the base of the box to determine* *the chassis size. Some groups have already cut and stuck the wood – others will be doing this – the glue gun will only be used for this part of the task – otherwise ordinary glue will be used – which means that they will have to leave things to set – consequently it is unlikely that there will be a completed model today. The children will also have to measure and cut the axles and choose the appropriate size of wheels. Information sheets provided as before – hopefully some group co-operation!*

Follow-up lessons: *Once the individual models were completed, these same mixed ability groups worked together in other areas of the curriculum using the models as a starting point. Each child wrote an account of how the model had been made. They worked together as a group with the computer and printer to get a printed account of how to make the chassis and wheels; as a group they produced graphs of how far each model would travel on different surfaces and how far they would travel using different slopes. For all these activities the children worked together in cooperation.'*

The descriptions below show how these lessons were tackled by the children.

Session 1: A group model

The group tackle their task with enthusiasm but with little evidence of planning – indeed children seem to grab for the materials that interest them most. In particular, the two boys are keen to start on the practical activity.

David: I'm doing the sawing [instantly followed by . . .]
Paul: I'll do a bit of sawing.

However, Jane is more appreciative of the need to organise the group and she turns to the instructions laid on their table. She takes on the role of group leader and since she is the only one who reads the instructions fully, it is only she who knows exactly what has to be done. She delegates tasks accordingly, sharing out the work, ensuring that Paul has his turn and that different children are drawn together. She is presumably responding to the helplessness of Paul who says after a few moments: 'I don't know what to do' and Hayley who asks, 'What am I doing?'

We see Jane talking generally to the group:

> Stacey can do the other bit.
> Paul and Stacey can do the next bit of sawing.
> Let Paul and David do that.

and more specifically to individuals in relation to their activities:

Jane to David:	Make sure you add on 2 centimetres at each end.
to Stacey:	Cut it there. See if you can hold it there.
to David:	Measure it 20 centimetres.
to Stacey:	Only 4 [tubes] . . . you chopped all these up – all we needed was 4.
to Paul:	Now we need the triangles.

Thus, with Jane's guidance, the task is completed successfully and all the group members make a significant contribution.

Session 2: Individual models

The children again tackle this project with enthusiasm, except for Paul, the low achiever, who after a while asks, '*What are we doing?*' No-one offers information, so he watches the rest of the group at work and attempts a start himself. After twenty minutes he states: '*I can't do this.*' Jane gives him some help, but then turns back to her own model. It is clear that Paul is still unable to make real progress and eventually Jane asks, '*Shall I do it for you? Done it yet?*'

It is interesting that the children are more prone to argument when the co-operative demand of the task is removed. As they make their individual carts, there is a tendency to argue over materials, and although this always ends in a friendly manner, a competitive element emerges.

Jane:	Thanks. I need a saw. Can I have the saw please?
David:	Yes.
Jane:	Can you hurry up?
Stacey:	You always keep that saw for yourself.
David:	I do not.
Stacey:	Yes you do.
David:	I gave it to Jane, so don't say that. I did give it to you didn't I?
Stacey:	Yes, but then you didn't share it again.
David:	Look, I promise I will.

Jane: Use after you please Stacey?
Stacey: I got to cut a titchy bit off.
Jane: I got 2 bits to cut here.
Stacey: Hey, you just want the saw to yourself.
Paul: Could you just cut that titchy bit?
Jane: OK, right Paul.

Since the children now need the saw for their own personal progress, the demand for it is heavier and more important to each individual.

During this session there is certainly evidence of helping behaviour, but since the children are building individual models, they are generally more interested in their own task than in each other's. The shared context seems to be useful and supportive but is not essential, as for the group model. The teacher is concerned that much of the peer help given, although allowing group members to complete a task by telling and showing, does not further understanding. So Paul, although encouraged to be useful during the building of the group cart, is still at a great disadvantage; he was not helped to read the instructions during the first lesson and, in retrospect, he clearly did not understand the construction process. Jane's concern and offer to '*do it for you*' is a good example of a generous co-operative gesture which might still leave Paul in a state of confusion. It would be possible to conclude from this that groupwork is an inappropriate context to promote understanding in a low attaining child. Yet it is clear that Paul was involved in the group, that he made to feel part of the group and that he was being given an opportunity to observe more able problem-solvers at work. These features may be of particular importance as starting points for the involvement of a child who usually finds it difficult to participate in the classes' activities.

A second feature which differentiates the two lessons is the comparative lack of talk in this second session, perhaps inevitably, given the interest in the individual construction. The task itself did not demand talk in the same way. It is interesting that David's and Paul's input to the group remained proportionately constant; Jane's talk however dropped from 39 per cent to 23 per cent, presumably because she no longer needed to organise the group to work together; Stacey's talk, however, rose from 4 per cent to 23 per cent – perhaps she did not feel dominated by Jane, perhaps she felt confident in the task and able to help others. The first session also generated a higher proportion of questions – perhaps again because of the demand of the task to co-operate fully; the majority of these questions unfortunately remained unanswered, perhaps unheard, not understood or discarded as not being important or relevant. The extent to which this could be detrimental to learning or attitudes might be of concern.

The teacher remains positive in her approach and concludes:

'given the right task, children can help each other even if the help given is mainly what Bennett *et al.* (1984) describes as "lower order". At least, the teacher is not having to spend her time dealing with such "lower order" requests. Furthermore if children are given enough practice in real co-operative groupwork, more "high order" help may well result. In this particular instance, the sessions were very successful. I am not sure that my headteacher would approve of whole class learning situations throughout the day, although I have tended to undertake fewer activities at any one time. This in itself does seem to make classroom management easier. I do not find myself rushing from one activity to another with hardly a moment to think. Consequently I do have more time to talk to individuals, to listen and to watch what is going on.'

Summary

The models for co-operative tasks are presented once more in order to recap the anticipated ways in which children will react to each one.

Model 1: Working individually on identical tasks for an individual outcome

When clearly asked to co-operate (and when co-operation is encouraged and valued) it seems that children will work effectively together and that the group context is important to their progress. 'Copying' becomes 'sharing' and there is no real evidence of competition, though argument may occur over sharing materials in a practical task, since each individual will need resources for himself. However, children who finish before others seem automatically to turn towards those who need help.

Model 2: Working individually on 'jigsaw' elements for a joint outcome

The effect of this model is similar to the one above, but there is an additional demand for planning and organisation as a group, both at the beginning and end of the task, and possibly throughout. This model may be particularly useful since it allows for individual work and individual accountability and yet the need to co-operate is central, and also because it seems that 'planning' is something that young children find difficult.

Model 3: Working jointly on one task for a joint outcome

Full co-operation probably presents the most difficulties for children. Planning and organisation are central, and it is these areas that lead to the most argument and tension between children, especially during practical activities. It is difficult for the group to ensure that all members are fully involved, but even the youngest show sensitivity to this and strategies evolve to ensure participation. If co-operation is to be developed even in difficult circumstances, then, teachers suggest, it is important to continue providing tasks with a joint outcome. However, where children get on well, or are used to working together, personal relationships generally cease to be such a problem and effective problem-solving and learning are likely to occur.

The children's response to the differing social demands is clearly related (as the extracts of talk have shown throughout this section) to the quality of the cognitive output. Where co-operation fails, even if only momentarily, then group cohesion is lacking and the momentum of the group is lost for that period of time. Fortunately, many of the children are extremely skilful at overcoming such a problem and co-operation is usually reinstated. Although good co-operation does not automatically lead to quality in pupil response to the cognitive demand of a task, it is certainly a prerequisite for effective groupwork. Without co-operation, especially for models two and three, it is extremely difficult to satisfy the cognitive requirements. Yet, as we have shown, it is a two-way process at work, for if the cognitive demand is too hard, or children do not have enough background experience and knowledge to discuss or answer questions, then it is likely that the co-operative element will disintegrate.

6 Managing groupwork

In this chapter, two major features in the management of groupwork are discussed: first, general classroom management, which provides the context for effective ways of working and, second, the choosing of groups that are likely to co-operate successfully.

Classroom management

> 'If the institution of cooperative learning is not accompanied with an effective classroom management system, serious problems are likely to occur. In my experience the single most important but most neglected topic in cooperative learning is classroom management.' (Kagan, 1988)

The National Curriculum asks that teachers should set up different groups for different tasks and purposes. Our concern in this section is thus to shed some light on management factors that teachers ought to take into account when setting up groups for co-operative work. Since one of our major interests lies in the ways that teachers can reorganise their time, particularly so that assessment demands can be met, we generally recommend that all groups work on the same task at the same time, at least when resources allow. We have already shown in Chapter 3 that, when teachers use this organisational strategy, their management burden is eased, and demands and pressures on their time become fewer. There are two major reasons for this. First, when all children work on the same task, it is easier for the teacher to predict the kinds of problem that will emerge and to concentrate on their solution – rather than responding to the wide range of both procedural and cognitive demands that occur with individualised work, or when each group has a different task. Second, co-operative groupwork encourages children to take on more responsibility for their own work and the management of their own groups.

A management system which allows for a whole class to be working in groups at the same time and on the same task is one that we would want to encourage and develop. This does not mean that it is the only way in which groups should function, nor does it mean that it is the only management system that should be adopted. However, for that part of the curriculum which lends itself to co-operative groupwork, it is a system which enables teachers to focus clearly on the content of a task, and to be specifically prepared for the kinds of materials, questions, problems, and so on which emerge from that one task. This, in turn, means that they are likely to be better prepared to cope with pupil demands. It is also a system which is designed to ease the complexities of management and is most likely to give teachers time for observation or assessment.

Kagan (1988), an American, stresses the importance of managing the structure and sequence of groupwork lessons, especially since he believes that teachers will have to rethink their management strategies.

'There are two major topics to cover with regard to managing the cooperative classroom: (1) managing student behaviour and (2) managing the structure and sequence of the lesson. In both areas, classroom management differs radically from classroom management in the traditional classroom.'

The changes demanded of American teachers may be more drastic than those needed in British classrooms. Kagan describes a scene to summarise the situation as he perceives it.

'It has become second nature to most teachers to exert energy keeping students quiet and attending only to the teacher or text. Teachers forget that they are demanding that students not do what they most want to do – interact with their peers. It is no wonder that teachers maintaining a traditional classroom end up so exhausted. They are bucking the basic nature of the student. Students want to question, discuss, argue and share. It is the great strength of cooperative learning that it channels this natural intelligence toward positive academic and social outcomes. In the process, however, great energy is released among students and the effective cooperative learning teacher must know how to manage a classroom of teams.'

In British primary classrooms, however, teachers are well used to children being seated in groups and rearrangement of furniture for co-operative work will seldom be necessary. In addition, teachers have allowed and encouraged talking for many years, so that noise level is unlikely to be a feature of concern. In other areas of management, changes will need to be similar on both sides of the Atlantic, particularly with regard to the teacher's role. Kagan emphasises how, in more traditional lessons, teachers provide an input which is followed by individual practice or application; for co-operative learning, the lessons may become structurally more complex – with both pupils and teacher assuming different roles in different parts of the lesson.

Although our own research suggests that teachers rarely set up groupwork in which all children tackle the same task at the same time, as is automatically assumed by Kagan, it is not actually a new idea. For example, Wynne Harlen (1985) provides a schematic way for thinking through flexible approaches to co-operative groupwork in science. She examines both teacher and pupil roles at different 'stages' of a lesson or topic, and shows how groupwork is just one of several kinds of learning context which needs support from other contributions. During each stage, the nature of interactions will be different and children will be involved in different kinds of activity.

Harlen provides a set of symbols to describe management possibilities (Figure 6.1). Harlen applies these symbols to four different kinds of

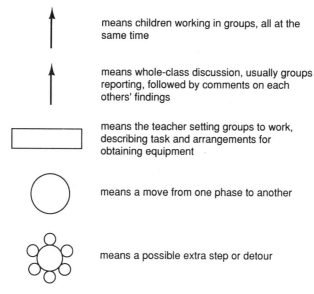

Figure 6.1

'topic' in science; one example is given below to demonstrate how co-operative groupwork is part of a whole system of management. The particular sequence is one that she sees as appropriate for questions such as: 'Which detergent washes the clothes best?'; 'Which polish is best for shining shoes?' and so on, but could be adapted to many other circumstances. A useful sequence for these topics allows children to work out how to decide which is 'best' during an initial period of free interaction with the materials (Figure 6.2).

This system of planning for the requirements of individual tasks is useful when thinking through the general organisation and management

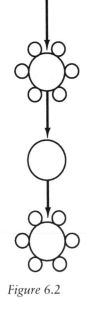

Teacher sets the scene, briefly describes problem of deciding 'which is best?'

Groups have equipment to explore and use while defining what 'best' means, what they have to do to decide it and what tests are necessary. A group record of their suggestions is drawn up.

Suggestions are collected from groups on the blackboard or large sheets of paper. Comments are invited about whether the suggested tests will show what they are intended to show, whether one test will be enough to decide 'best', etc. In some cases tests may already have been carried out roughly; suggestions should be made for improvement. Ways of recording results discussed.

Children carry out tests (probably different ones by each group or similar ones carried out in different ways). Teacher reminds them about recording helps by showing techniques where necessary.

Groups' results reported to others, possibly by demonstrating what was done and showing results already drawn up in a table, graph or chart. Discussion of meaning of results, whether enough testing done to justify selection of 'best', etc. Critical review leading to suggestions for improvement.

Groups act on suggestions for extending and improving tests. May modify results and conclusions. Possible preparation of classroom display of results.

Figure 6.2

of lessons. Surprisingly, this kind of overall planning, even at its most simple level, may not frequently occur. For example, the use of class follow-up or reporting back sessions may not be widespread. In Kerry and Sands (1983), it is stated:

'I did not see one lesson where there was a follow-up so that children could pool experience. I felt that this was one of the major weaknesses of the group work I saw. A follow-up would have been useful and helpful for the children for two important reasons:

1 to pool experience of work which had gone well or badly.
2 to revise and link together aspects of the whole topic when each group had been working on slightly different activities.'

The power of a system which is dependent on reporting back, sharing activities, knowledge, ideas and so on, both with the teacher and other class members, is inevitably lost if different groups are working in different curriculum areas or on completely different subject content. However, co-operative groupwork is likely to be most effective when used as part of a whole series of activities and part of a co-operative process involving the whole class.

Further, and more specific, aspects of management, including the extent to which teachers should involve themselves in groups, and the management of pupil demands, are discussed in Chapter 7, in the context of training for groupwork skills. Before training can take place, decisions must obviously be made about the best ways to divide the class into groups that have a real potential for working together.

Choosing groups

'For myself, as the teacher, the major difficulty was the initial choosing of the groups. It was necessary to take into account the children's ability, sex and personality.'

Eggleston and Kerry (1988) suggest that setting up groups needs serious attention; a learning tool which has great potential may not be effectively utilised, they say, since teachers do not have efficient knowledge of group dynamics. They are, however, fully aware of a central problem:

'... in a typical class of top juniors there may be six years difference between the reading ages of the ablest and least able readers; and other abilities will be similarly disparate. For this reason, and because the whole philosophy of the mixed-ability class seems to run counter to grouping by ability, teachers are often at a loss to know how to assign pupils to working groups.'

When setting up groupwork, one of the major questions to be addressed has to be: 'What is the best way to arrange the groups?' This is a question for which it is not easy to provide a cut-and-dried response since few studies have directly investigated the problem. Indeed Biott (1984) concluded that it is impossible to opt for any one best composition for groups, since 'decisions about grouping a class will have to be made in a specific context. No generalised strategy is appropriate.'

There is, however, a growing body of research which has highlighted more appropriate or less appropriate features in terms of group size and composition, and details of these are outlined below.

Group size

In Britain, teachers tend to seat their pupils in groups of between four and six children (HMI, 1978; Bennett *et al.*, 1984); this pattern no doubt reflecting attempts to make the best use of space and furnishing constraints as well as curriculum resources. So far as co-operative groupwork is concerned, it remains difficult to give hard-and-fast rules about optimal size.

Biott (1984) suggests that there should be no fixed rules, with groups of three, four or five being satisfactory, since any decisions made will need to be dependent on the classroom context. In contrast to this, Kagan (1988) is very clear about group size, since it will have a marked impact on the opportunity for, and the nature of, children's interactions. He points out that the number of children in a group will determine the number of lines of communication and hence states: 'Teams of four are ideal. A team of three is often a dyad and an outsider; in a team of three there are three possible lines of communication; in a team of four there are six. Doubling the lines of communication increases learning potential . . . Teams of five often leave an odd man out and leave less time for individual participation.'

When this is shown in diagrammatic form (Figure 6.3), it becomes instantly clear that the impact of group size is inevitably great and that a group of four will allow for a range of possibilities without making the 'lines of communication' too complex. For our own research, a team of teachers in one school spent the best part of a year experimenting with group size and reported that, in their experience, teams of four

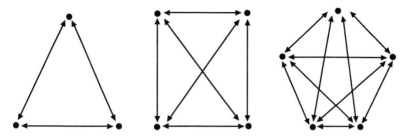

Figure 6.3 Lines of communication in groups of three to five pupils

did seem to be the most effective. The National Oracy Project (1990) also suggest that groups of four can be used as a strategy for developing co-operation:

> 'As a generalization, younger and quieter children seem to do better in pairs than in larger groups. A useful strategy is to start children off in friendship pairs and then put two pairs together to share what they have done. This means that each pair has a contribution to make.'

There is a good deal of evidence that pairs of children will work well together (see the ever-increasing literature on peer-tutoring; eg, Topping (1988)) but in our own research we have not used pairs.

As a generalisation, it does seem that groups of three and four are the most likely to co-operate to good purpose; that groups of five may divide into a dyad and a trio, or may allow individuals to opt out; and that larger groups will certainly split up into smaller groupings, with the possibility of opting out made far more likely.

Group composition

Free-choice and friendship groups

Many teachers allow free-choice or friendship groups, at least for work in some curriculum areas (though seldom for maths, where ability – or attainment – groups are preferred). Rosen and Rosen (1973) are clear in their commitment to friendship groups:

> 'I would not wish to draw an idealized picture of childhood, and, indeed, the many quarrels and arguments are an important and necessary part of growing up and language learning, however inconvenient or distressing they may be in a classroom with a large group of children. Nevertheless, a freer flowing of children allowing them to form their own groups for

working together does at least create the conditions for greater cooperation, for joint effort in a common enterprise, and more important still, the possibility of nurturing empathy and understanding between them.'

The National Oracy Project (1990) provide an account from a head of an infant school, stating that this account is a summary of what they are aiming for, with talk having 'its rightful place in the curriculum and in the eyes of pupils and teachers':

> '"My school has placed an emphasis on oracy over several years, with all staff involved. Children have used talk in lots of different ways and discussed its effectiveness. The result is that teachers no longer have to put children into groups. When a child has a piece of work to do you may hear them say "I need a partner to talk this through" or "I think a group of us should work on this together" or "I'm going to have a go at this on my own. When I've got a draft I'll discuss it with you (teacher)". They use talk as a tool for learning like reading, writing or observing."'

This kind of flexible approach to grouping may be useful and it may be particularly appropriate for infants, for some part of the day, or in particular curriculum areas; we would stress, however, that more formal attention to group composition will allow for different kinds of interaction. Children who are always encouraged to choose their grouping, or are always allowed to work with friends, will not necessarily extend beyond a narrow range of possibilities. There will, therefore, be no necessary obligation for tolerance or patience with children who would not normally get on together, nor necessarily any need for children of either like, or dissimilar, abilities to work alongside each other – both of which might be important for social and cognitive development. For this reason we advocate, at least from time to time, a more planned approach to group composition.

An issue commonly raised is that, if the teacher determines the composition of the group, children could end up with others they do not like. However, since one of the social purposes of groupwork is to overcome prejudices, pupils should, at least on occasion, be persuaded to work at group relationships despite personal likes or dislikes. In the words of Kagan (1988): 'The power of team-building, class-building, and positive group dynamics draws initially hostile and reluctant students into full participation.'

One teacher in our study described how friendship patterns were changed in her own classroom when, alongside the ability groups and friendship groups which she had customarily organised, she included mixed-ability groups in the repertoire. Pupils who did not usually have any contact in academic terms were suddenly obliged to take notice of each other. After a few 'rough patches' it became clear that many of these contacts were either valued or tolerated, and that this, in turn, had an impact on friendship groups.

Attainment groups

All teachers will inevitably be faced with pupils in their classes who possess a wide range of academic and linguistic skills. Cohen (1986) reports that, in America, the methods for overcoming this problem have generally been the use of ability groups or individualised work. Her findings are very similar in nature to our own. She states: 'There is no evidence that ability grouping, particularly for those in low-ability groups, is effective (Hallinan, 1984), and the problems with giving seatwork assignments to students who are operating below grade level have already been emphasized.'

In our own work with teachers, there were very few occasions on which low attainers were allowed to work together in groups, but a few experimental situations were set up in order to test out the kinds of problem encountered by groups of low attaining children attempting to work on a co-operative task. The few teachers involved each reported that these particular groups were an enormous drain on their time at the expense of other children; that low attaining pupils showed little skill in encouraging and allowing the group to work together; that they found difficulty with interpreting the task and communicating any understanding purposefully. For these reasons, any co-operative activity that did occur failed to have an impact and the children were not drawn into the activity in the same way as when working with more able peers in a mixed ability group. One teacher states of the group interaction:

'Overall there was little explaining done, a low level of instructional talk and infrequent suggestions, so that the pupils gained very little academically from each other.'

Another teacher says of a low attaining group: 'It was a case of the blind leading the blind. Nobody was capable of questioning the mistakes they were making.'

A group of low attainers who had been asked to represent a car survey in graph form were monitored carefully. It appeared that the larger group broke into three sub-groups, each working separately and with little interaction and the end-product came in the form of three separate graphs rather than a single presentation. Their teacher observes:

> 'As no-one had taken the role of leader or was acting as a peer tutor these problems were not overcome without teacher intervention. When the other members of the group were asked by the teacher to help Wendy and Michelle, they were willing and able to do so but there had been no previous assistance offered. Michelle and Wendy are both introverted pupils and they had not discussed their work within the group. Studies in America by Webb (1982) have shown that introverted pupils are less likely to receive explanations in response to errors than extroverted pupils, and there is evidence here of this happening.'

She rightly asks the question whether the task was too difficult or unstructured for members of this group. She decides, however:

> 'I do not consider that it was, as when I encouraged group co-operation the information that Michelle and Wendy needed was provided by other members of the group. The weakness appeared to be within the group structure rather than within the task.'

Two of the boys in this group failed to complete their graphs and there was no attempt at a group summary of the survey. Yet low attainers attempting the same task in the same classroom, but who were involved in mixed ability groups, gave evidence of being enabled to work more successfully through co-operative interaction with more able peers. Another teacher describes a similar situation, concluding:

> 'The low attaining group remained on task much more than was expected but produced little and the work was of poor quality with multiple errors, due to the poor leadership within the group, lack of planning, lack of accurate assistance with low level requests, etc.'

From this evidence we cannot conclude that groups of low attaining children should never be allowed to work together; there may well be a time and a purpose for this and it may, on occasion, prove successful. However, teachers should bear in mind that, if such groups are set up, they must be prepared to give disproportionate amounts of time and support to these pupils.

An alternative strategy to the use of homogenous groups is obviously that of heterogeneous groups, with less able group members learning from the more able, where skills are shared and where co-operative interpretation of the task allows all to understand what is expected.

Johnson and Johnson (1985), the most prolific researchers on co-operative groupwork in America, suggest that: 'one of the important internal dynamics of co-operative learning groups may be the opportunity for students with differing achievement histories to interact with one another . . .' Further to this, Cohen (1986) argues:

> 'If each group member is required to turn out a product demonstrating understanding but is allowed to use resources in the group to achieve that understanding, the student with weak academic skills will not sit back and go along with the group. If the task is challenging and interesting, he or she will become actively engaged and will demand assistance and explanation. For students more advanced in academic skills, the act of explaining to others represents one of the finest ways to solidify their own learning . . . In review, if students are properly prepared, heterogeneous groups can represent a solution to one of the most persistent problems of classroom teaching . . . Lack of skills in reading, writing and computation need not bar students from exposure to lessons requiring conceptualisation. At the same time, these students can develop their basic skills with assistance from their classmates.'

This kind of argument leads inevitably to a new question: 'Do high attainers suffer in mixed ability groups?' Teachers on both sides of the Atlantic are concerned about high attainers in heterogeneous groups. Kagan (1988) expresses their discomfort in the following question, which he then answers.

> 'Isn't the accelerated achievement of low achieving students in cooperative learning bought at the expense of high achieving students? Couldn't the high achievers learn more if they were not stuck tutoring . . .?'
> 'The question surprises me coming from teachers. As teachers, we know that we continually learn more about the topics we teach in the process of teaching others. As we tutor, even simple questions from the tutee make us look at our subject matter freshly. As we try to determine the easiest way to convey understanding or overcome a learning block, we ourselves gain a deeper understanding of our topic. But then, somehow, we deny that deeper understanding to our students. We do not let them teach. When we look at our students, we forget our own experience and how much teaching is itself a great teacher.'

Kagan believes that we tend to interpret teaching in too narrow a sense, without considering the kinds of motivation that can be provided by groupwork and the opportunities for tutoring that are likely to emerge spontaneously among peers. In addition, he states that high achievers will learn far more than academic content in a co-operative context: 'Leadership skills, self-esteem gains, conflict-resolution skills, and role-taking abilities are part of the "new curriculum" included along with cooperative learning.'

There seems to be no doubt that high attaining children are often involved in all kinds of organising activities within their groups, both in terms of the co-operative demands of the tasks and the cognitive content. We now consider some examples of high achievers involved in such activity and investigate in some depth the kinds of skills they bring to a co-operative situation.

Thomas

Thomas is a ten-year-old who takes on a leadership role in his group and raises the standard of work considerably, skilfully encouraging, questioning and organising. He is one of a mixed ability group of five children who have collected data for the class survey of cars. Their teacher reports in detail:

> '... the groups had to decide upon different mathematical ways of showing their findings. In this group, Thomas ensured that a number of different methods were used. After finding out from Carley and Vanessa that they wanted to draw a bar graph he then told David and Nathan that they could do a pie-chart. The two boys readily agreed to this although it is unlikely that they would have been able to construct a pie-chart without help. Thomas gave Andrew the chance to choose and agreed to his suggestion of percentages but then added "If we do a line graph as well as percentages it'll make it better." Thus, in this group, four different methods of showing the pupils' findings were being used.

As the lesson progressed, the role of peer tutor, which Thomas had taken upon himself, become more marked as the following conversation between him and Carley illustrates:

Thomas: How many colours have you got? You've got 1, 2, 3 . . . 9, 10. So if you write the colours along the bottom, and the numbers like 1, 1, 1. No, no, like 0, 5, 10, 15, 20 like that up the side. No, maybe less.

Carley: Do we have to do it in 2s then?

Thomas: Yes . . . in 4s might be better.

Carley: 4, 8 . . .

Thomas: No, in 2s probably as it only goes up to 40.

Carley: Oh, yes.

Thomas: OK, right that will best. So you've got that. Just write the colours, there's 1, 2, 3 . . . 9 colours.

Thomas planned the best way of drawing the graph as if it had been his own piece of work. Whilst he asked questions of Carley – "How many colours have you got?", he answered the question by counting the colours himself. Carley and Vanessa had not asked for assistance from Thomas and, in fact, drawing a bar graph was a familiar task for them so that they could almost certainly have done without help. The fact that Carley suggested doing it in 2's showed that she understood the idea of appropriate scale in graph work. However, the girls appeared to be happy to accept Thomas' advice and were content after this conversation to draw the graph as Thomas had suggested. In a similar way, Thomas supervised the making of a pie-chart by Nathan and David, even suggesting that they could "go outside and spot one more manual (gearbox)" in order to bring the number of cars they counted to 40 so that it would be easier to divide the pie-chart. (This is a good example of pupils using adaptive learning strategies in order to make the task easier to accomplish.) At the same time he was leading Andrew in their own task of producing a line graph and giving the percentages for cars from different countries of manufacture. When anyone in the group was having a problem, either in interpreting their information or in deciding how to present their findings, Thomas offered assistance. It appeared that he was able to do his own element of the task at the same time as listening to and helping the other members of the group. Whilst the pupils were working on different elements of the task they were held together as a group by the overview of Thomas.'

The group's talk related only to their task, and despite members dividing into sub-groups for production purposes, there was constant interaction between them in order to fulfil the co-operative requirements. They discussed the various stages of the activity, including, as is shown below, the summary and final prediction. The extract of talk presented below demonstrates that Thomas enabled all the children to be involved at this stage, whereas if the group had consisted only of the less able members they would not have had sufficient knowledge or understanding to do so. The extract is annotated with suggestions as to the type of activity in which Thomas is involved as he talks with the rest of his group.

Thomas:	Now, the summary and the prediction. So how do you reckon we should write the summary?	*Questions*
Nathan:	I don't know.	
David:	Nathan doesn't know.	
Vanessa:	Nor does David.	
Thomas:	Come on, think. OK, get Painer	

	[ie, Andrew] to do it, alright.	*Admonishes*
Andrew:	What?	
David:	What are you going to do Painer?	
Andrew:	I don't know.	
Thomas:	OK, you can do that Carley.	*Allocates*
Carley:	Eh?	
Thomas:	The summary of what we've learned.	*Repeats*
Carley:	We've learnt about cars.	
Thomas:	No, no, you've got to work out from what you get.	*Rephrases*
David:	If we collect all our information together we could say how many red automatic cars there are and how many red manual cars there were.	
Carley:	Yes.	
Thomas:	On average from the number of cars we predicted we'll take the smallest number of cars found.	
Carley:	Right, yes.	
Thomas:	We can try it. [To Carley] If you do the summary. If Carley writes the summary from the information that we all give her. What about the prediction? What do you see as the prediction? What does she [the teacher] mean by prediction?	*Allocates and Summarises Questions Rephrases*
Nathan:	A guess?	
Thomas:	A guess of what?	*Probes*
Nathan:	Let's go a bit further than a guess. Is that what it means – let's go a bit further than a guess?	
Vanessa:	An estimate.	
Thomas:	Yes. We'll do the prediction after the summary.	*Accepts Answer and Organises*

The teacher summarises:

'Without Thomas' guidance it seems very unlikely that anyone would have volunteered to write either the summary or the prediction or that the other group members would have known what was involved in doing these.'

Furthermore, it seems that Thomas is practising important skills himself, as well as enabling others to achieve. He shows sensitivity and a concern for understanding in others; group leadership allows him to develop these aspects of co-operative working at the same time as restructuring his mathematical knowledge by making use of it in a new context. Although he might be seen as over-dominant, the children do respond well to him, show no resentment and certainly produce work of a higher quality than they would otherwise have managed.

Sarah

Let us now look at the role that Sarah plays when asked for help by Louise. Sarah is an eight-year-old and academically the most confident of her group who are constructing triangular prisms. Her teacher states:

'Sarah is the only member of the group to explain and begin to show in her talk elements of "guiding participation".'

Rachael: Sarah can you help me?
Sarah: How?
Rachael: Because every time I pick a number it won't work out.
Sarah: How do you mean?
Rachael: Right, I pick a number and I go down here . . . that goes up to there and that's half way down, isn't it?
Sarah: You've done that bit wrong. That's it up to there and that's half way down isn't it? So it needs to go up there and then your triangle comes across here. Doesn't it? And then you come down one, two . . . six. You come down six there.

Throughout Sarah is checking that Rachael is following her explanation, she is also providing a bridge between what Rachael has done and what she perceives as the next step for Rachael. The support continues a minute later with:

Sarah: Right, so your triangle's here, draw it on. Draw a straight line like that . . . a straight line across . . . make sure it's straight . . . that's it . . . now, draw along the edges . . .

now how many do you want across? [A few seconds later she provides further encouragement in a different style.] Come on then, draw. [Sarah watches.] Now get your ruler and draw across. [Rachael is still showing she has difficulties.] . . . so you'll have to do it down . . . exactly the same as you did there.

On one occasion, as soon as Sarah has finished speaking, Rachael uses her exact words. It appears that in copying Sarah's talk she is trying to gain a clear understanding of the process.

Sarah: That one goes over like that . . . and that one sticks onto there and you need one on that one.

Rachael: Yeah that's right . . . and that one sticks onto there and you need one on that one . . . wait there, wait there, I've done that bit wrong.

Rachael clearly benefitted from this help and the teacher points out that Sarah, though very able, is a child who finds it difficult to make long-term friends. For this reason, the experience of explaining and demonstrating in a co-operative context might be of particular importance socially as well as academically.

Louise
There is also evidence that a high attainer can dominate talk in such a way that others, who are less able to participate easily in discussion and are slow to phrase ideas, may be virtually excluded. Louise plays a useful part in her group in that she is willing and able to answer all the task-related questions posed by the others. However, Donna tends to talk in incomplete utterances and many of her questions are ignored. The teacher is concerned:

'Donna may be overwhelmed, so that she is not so confident to try the next time.'

Donna: And if we have . . .
Louise: A cup of tea Mum will drink it.
Donna: Yea, in case . . .
Louise: Because when the flowers are in the vase . . .

If her talk is anticipated and more dominant children take the lead in talk, then her questions remain unanswered and she receives little reward for attempting conversation. Much of her talk appears to be disregarded by the others. Also, she gets muddled about the character's names and the other children become quite impatient with her:

Donna: Dan's a girl, Dan's a girl, isn't she?
Alan: No!
Anna: No!
Louise: No, Dan's a boy! ... Kim's a girl ... that's not Kim!

It would be very difficult for a teacher to pick up this kind of exclusion of a child unless the group's talk was taped; taping on just one occasion would highlight with which children this is likely to occur. It is also important, in this instance, to know that Louise is only seven years old, and it might therefore be expected that children of this age are not fully sensitive to the needs of others for support and patience in listening.

For those who remain concerned as to the value of mixed ability groups for the high attainer, a research study by Bennett and Cass (1988) has recently shown that the most able children perform well no matter what group composition is used. The concern of the study is again, above all, for the less able, who do not always fare so well. For example, when children were sitting in groups of three and when two high attainers were grouped with one low attainer it was not a satisfactory experience for the latter. The two able children talked together but tended to ignore the less able child, who was unable to follow their conversation. On the other hand, when one high attainer was grouped with two lower attainers it was generally a great success, with the former taking a tutoring role, supporting the others with knowledge, ideas and explanations. This suggests, perhaps, that the highest attainers should be shared around a class. It was also found that homogeneous groups of low attainers or of average attainers consistently performed the worst.

Although the American research has reached slightly different conclusions (see Webb *et al.*, 1986) there is enough overlap to reinforce the implications for group composition. Webb found, for example, that the best results were obtained when high attainers were spread across groups, since if they were left together there was a general lack of co-operation, the feeling being that it was unnecessary. Webb also found that low attainers did little explaining, suggesting (as has been seen elsewhere) that they did not possess enough knowledge of the subject matter, or skills in that area, to give effective explanations. Overall, her arguments give support for mixed ability groups.

Boys and girls

Much research shows that the gender effeect is pronounced in classroom groups, whether or not the grouping is co-operative. Galton *et al.* (1980), for example, showed that over 80 per cent of conversations were between members of the same sex, whether or not children were seated in mixed sex groups. Other British research on co-operating groups shows that mixed sex groups can be unproductive. Unfortunately, different research suggests that all-girl groups tend to be very consensus oriented, that is, concerned to seek agreement and reduce tension so that children do not probe and challenge each other (see Tann, 1980).

A major consideration when setting up groups is whether to opt for single or mixed sex groups. If we asked primary-aged children for their opinions about this, many comments such as the following could be expected:

Teacher: If I said you could work in groups of all girls, or just boys, or a few girls and a few boys, which would you choose?
Jacky: All girls.
Teacher: Why's that?
Jacky: Because boys are horrible and girls are nice.
Teacher: Why are boys horrible?
Jacky: Because they always shout.

The teacher who asked the above questions was interested in her class's perceptions of working together and, in particular, their preferences for gender within the groups. Some of the responses from individual children are given below. Belinda and Claudia had been working in all-girl groups; Simon had been working with other boys.

Teacher: So if you could choose a group to work with, would you choose all boys, all girls or a few girls and a few boys?
Belinda: Just girls.
Teacher: Why would you choose all girls?
Belinda: Because I can't work with boys.
Teacher: Why not?
Belinda: Because they try to tell me what to do.

Simon: Just boys.
Teacher: Do you know why?
Simon: Cos they're not fussy.

Claudia: Boys try to take over it. They say 'take that bit down' and things like that.

Teacher: In all group work or just when you're working with construction toys?
Claudia: They'd just do it with construction.
Teacher: Why's that?
Claudia: They think they're better at it. When I'm working with them on the Bauspiel [construction material] they take over it all. They say 'I think I do better stuff than you'.

In the following two extracts from the interviews, Kate and Ian show satisfaction with working in a mixed group.

Teacher: Did you think you all worked well as a group?
Ian: Yes. Well sometimes Amanda wasn't very good, or Kate.
Teacher: Did you all share your ideas?
Ian: Yeah.
Teacher: Did anyone try to take over?
Ian: No.
Teacher: Do you think anyone got left over?
Ian: Sometimes, I think, when Amanda stopped, and Kate, I think they got a bit left out.
Teacher: Who had the best ideas in the group?
Ian: Um. [15-second pause] I don't know.
Teacher: If I said to you: 'Which would you rather work with, all other girls, all boys or a few girls and a few boys, what would you say?'
Ian: A few boys and a few girls.

Teacher: Who had the best ideas in the group?
Kate: [5-second pause] Um, I think Ian.
Teacher: So would you rather work in groups made up of girls, all boys or a few boys and a few girls?
Kate: A few girls and a few boys.

Interestingly, both of these two children had been working in a mixed sex group of four, whereas the others had been in all-girl or all-boy groups. Could their satisfaction with a mixed group stem simply from this experience? Can prejudice be avoided by asking mixed groups to co-operate and by building on these positive experiences? It is clear that while Ian and Kate were constructing their shelter, the whole group was involved in a good deal of task-related and co-operative talk between the sexes and across the group, as shown by Figure 6.4. The girls talked slightly less than the boys and least of all to each other. Several teachers who had previously allowed friendship groups

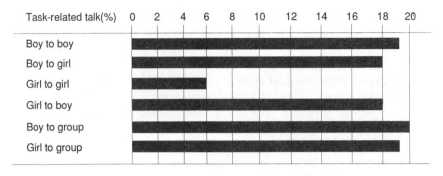

Figure 6.4 Comparisons of amounts of talk in a mixed-sex group

in their infant classrooms, and these groups invariably being single sex, decided to test out what happened when they created mixed sex groups. These teachers were interested by their findings which generally supported each other; to take two examples:

'The children interacted freely with the opposite sex and so I would surmise that, although children of this age often **choose** to interact with the same sex, they are equally happy in a mixed group.'

'During my career I have observed that children generally group themselves by gender and these single sex groups usually worked harmoniously. Since undertaking this research, I have realised that in fact the children in these single sex groups, which appeared to be working so well, might have been learning a great deal more from each other had they been in mixed sex groups.'

At the secondary level, Cowie and Ruddock (1988) suggest that there are real difficulties with implementing mixed sex groupings; as an example they say that girls may not feel confident enough to contribute, in a teacher's words, 'for fear of the ridicule and hostility of the boys.' They believe that 'educators face a great challenge in attempting to overcome deeply-rooted gender bias.'

Webb (1987) shows concern about the mixture of gender within a group, though her focus is mainly on 'explanation'. She reports:

'The mixture of gender in a group also influences who obtains explanations. One study showed that in groups with equal numbers of girls and boys, all students seem to obtain help when they ask for it. In contrast, when boys outnumber girls or when girls outnumber boys (particularly when there is only one girl or one boy in a group), the boys are more successful than girls in obtaining help. In groups with mostly boys, the girl is often ignored. In groups with mostly girls, the girls direct many of their questions to the boys, who tend not to answer all their questions.'

It does seem that there is a developmental trend in the relationships between boys and girls. Whereas at the infant level the sexes do seem to interact readily with each other when given the opportunity, and this is also the case through much of the junior age-range, there is an increasing tendency for negative relationships to develop, and these perhaps reach a peak in the early secondary years. However, what we do not know is whether children who have been encouraged to work co-operatively over a long period of time would react in the same ways, or whether attitudes might be changed.

As yet we have insufficient evidence to know whether children in single sex or mixed sex groups are able to learn more effectively or to produce better work. Thus there is a dilemma for the teacher of both a moral and an organisational kind – should boys and girls be grouped together as a matter of principle to fulfil both social and academic goals, even if the children prefer otherwise? Our own belief is that they should, at least some of the time, but this is an issue which each teacher must resolve to their own satisfaction.

It has already been suggested in our research findings that the content of the task may have an impact on the kind of language used by boys and by girls (see Chapter 3). A sequence of three tasks performed by the same group but in different curriculum areas demonstrates a marked example of other ways in which the subject area may influence interaction between boys and girls.

(a) **Task 1 – maths**. The group of four nine-year-old children (three boys and one girl) are given a sheet of outline hexagons; these are to be sub-divided with first one, then two, then three lines to see how many different shapes can be made (see Figure 6.5).

Ian: A line across there will make two trapeziums.
Barry: A line from there to the middle and across.
Sarah: That makes two trapeziums.

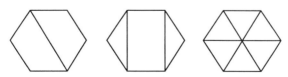

Figure 6.5 Ways to sub-divide hexagons

Barry: A line from top left to bottom left . . .
Sarah: And you've got a pentagon and a triangle . . . If you put a line from there to the middle one – oh no, just done that.

The two boys and Sarah seem here to be co-operating and talking easily together; Sarah could perhaps be considered as fairly dominant. Tom, the third boy, participates little in any talk, though he does appear to be involved in the tasks.

(b) **Task 2 – technology.** The same children are building a 'brick' tower.

Barry: I'll do it, I'll do it.
Ian: Me and Barry ought to do it.
Ian: No, me and Tom will.
Barry: You and Tom do it.
Ian: I think I'd better measure it, it's going to fall in a minute.
Sarah: What am I supposed to do then?
Sarah: [with raised voice] What shall I do then?
Barry: Nothing.

Sarah goes away to build her own tower:

Ian: She'll never do it. Me and Tom and Barry are best.

(c) **Task 3 – English.** The children are now writing a story together.

Barry: So now we can start writing the story.
Sarah: But what we have got to do is find out how to spell 'aborigine'. Shall I get a dictionary?
Barry: OK. You get a dictionary out.

Sarah now seems to be in favour again, the competitive element has gone and Sarah does not show any signs of long-term resentment after her treatment during the technology task.

A further curriculum area which may determine the way in which boys and girls approach a task is when they work at computers. One headteacher states:

'In a quick survey involving two thirds of our school, I asked two teachers to send their classes in groups of three, mixed sex, throughout

the day to work at a simple computer game. No matter how they came in, GIRL GIRL BOY or BOY BOY GIRL, etc., the central seat and mastery of the keyboard was taken by a boy.
Only twice was the hot seat taken by the girl. Out of the two incidences one girl sat in the middle but the boy on her left leaned over and did all the button pushing. The other girl was in complete control of the keyboard as a very high attainer with two very low attaining males.'

A particular girl who was specifically watched also provided an interesting case study.

'The girl in our research had mainly secretarial skills assigned to her by the boys during the on-computer stage and yet off-computer she assumed a leadership role in organising the production of the log book. The boys did not always take her advice but they did listen more when off computer than when on.'

We do not know whether this is a scenario often encountered, but suggest that teachers do watch out for similar situations, and if possible redress the balance, since, 'this is an area when classroom organisation could enhance the learning opportunities of girls by positive discrimination, and actually directing them on to the keyboard.'

Children's personality

'The personalities of some of the members of the groups had as much, if not more, effect on the functioning of the group than their ability.'

The personality of individual children is a feature that teachers seriously consider when deciding on group composition. Below, three teachers describe how they choose their groups, personality being one of several factors that they take into account.

Teacher A

'I decided to mix boys and girls in the groups . . .
I decided to mix junior with top infants, and top infants with middle infants, otherwise the age range might be too wide . . .
I had to consider the children's personalities together with age and ability.
Several of the junior children were quite shy, while there were a number of children with assertive personalities . . .'

Teacher B

'I always tended to group children by ability, which usually leaves a group of low achievers who seem to demand a disproportionate amount of my time. For this particular study I made up heterogeneous groups with a low and a high achiever in each group and I also tried to ensure that there was a child in each group who could think "creatively", someone who might be able to provide ideas.'

Teacher C

'I have become very aware in the course of my investigations that the dynamics of groups plays a major role in their effectiveness. It is not just a case of mixed ability, homogeneous or heterogeneous groupings. The personalities of the children involved, the activities they are given to do, even the time of day, have their effect on how the group operates ... much thought needs to be given when organising groups. Thus the teacher needs to know the children's abilities very well, subject by subject, as a high performer in maths may not be so in language. It also points to the usefulness of grouping to split up children of similar ability who may be in friendship groups and would not normally choose to work with different ability children. The children obviously prefer to work in friendship groups, but many respond well to being "arranged" into different groups.'

The range of criteria shows that teachers are sophisticated in their judgements. Although personality clearly plays a central role, it is difficult to generalise about effects and teachers themselves are in the best position to make decisions in the light of their own knowledge about the particular pupils in their class.

When reviewing groupwork in their own classrooms, teachers tend to focus on the more negative aspects on personality, for example, children who are over-dominant:

'This was not a happy working group. The authoritarian, impatient attitude of the group leader and the conflicts experienced between her and another child prevented a level of rapport necessary for genuine cooperative efforts, and one girl was very much excluded.'

Another teacher describes how two boys caused a real problem for her:

'Two boys in particular seemed unable to consider the ideas of others and wanted their way only. It is these two boys who consistently cause problems in group activities. Yet if we could find ways for the other children to accept them, the boost to their confidence would surely change their attitude. This is the real challenge to me as their teacher because to continue working on group activities emphasises the fact that the other children shun these two boys, so making it worse for them than if they were all working on individual tasks.'

In another class, one boy was extremely unpopular and 'constantly picked on'; he was frequently not accepted into group activities and other children seemed irritated by his presence in a group. The class teacher was unable to assess specifically what personality features provoked this lack of acceptance, but eventually decided that it was his lack of willingness to be involved and his lack of effort, even when others gave him every opportunity to participate, that made them angry.

We consider 'negative behaviour' in more detail in Chapter 7 on training – as well as discussing ways in which some of these problems might be overcome. It is important to remember, however, that many personality traits of children are extremely positive; all kinds of helpful behaviours and examples of patience and tolerance have already been examined in previous extracts of talk.

Summary

In terms of classroom management, we advocate that groups are involved in whole-class activities in order to maximise the potential of co-operative groupwork. In addition, the groupwork itself often needs to be part of a wider system of management which makes use of, for example, reporting back by groups to the whole class.

It is difficult to be specific about the optimal size and composition of groups. Groups of three to four children are likely to work well; mixed ability groups are likely to be of benefit to the widest range of pupils, with high attainers involving themselves in higher order skills both in terms of group management and cognitive development and other children benefitting from the ways in which they can be drawn into activities. Although we recommend mixed gender groups, and there is plenty of evidence that girls and boys can work effectively together, it is not possible to claim that children either learn or progress better in such groups. Teachers clearly consider personality features as central to decision-making about group composition.

7   Training in groupwork skills

In many American research studies of co-operative groupwork, a major feature is the way in which children are rewarded for working together. A series of incentives for pupils – in the form of team points, certificates and so on – are often used in the belief that it is these rewards which encourage pupils to work effectively together to complete their tasks (see Slavin, 1987).

Such incentives are unlikely to be a central motivating force in British classrooms. There is, however, an apparently widespread assumption that children will not only be prepared and willing to work co-operatively, but also that they will be able to do so without any particular difficulties. Yet further American research, especially that of Kagan (1988) and Cohen (1986), shows clearly that successful groupwork only occurs when teachers and pupils are made aware of the kinds of skills and behaviours that are central to its effective operation.

Kagan refers to training in co-operative skills as 'teambuilding' and states:

'The amount, type and timing of teambuilding depends on the needs and characteristics of the particular students, and the values of the teacher . . . Teambuilding creates enthusiasm, trust and mutual support which in the long run lead to more efficient academic work. If there are racial or other tensions, teambuilding is a must. To go on with cooperative learning without dealing with such tensions, in the long run will not work.'

He also specifically argues that, where heterogeneous groups have been formed by the teacher, teambuilding will be essential to overcome the almost inevitable problems. Kagan suggests a list of skills which he believes are crucial to effective groupwork, as well as certain behaviours which he considers to be destructive (or disfunctional). This list is briefly outlined below since it is useful in giving teachers ideas for the kind of activities which they can themselves encourage in groupwork. If children are to work effectively in groups, they will certainly need to take a lead from their teacher as prompt and guide. As Kagan says:

'For pupils to benefit from such work . . . requires a degree of tolerance and mutual understanding, the ability to articulate a point of view, to engage in discussion, reasoning, probing and questioning. Such skills are not in themselves innate, they have to be learnt and so taught.'

Kagan's suggestions for positive behaviours demonstrate a need for a certain amount of linguistic sophistication. Children should be able to be involved in: initiating activity; seeking information and opinions; giving information and opinions; elaborating; co-ordinating and summarising. At the same time, they should be aware of keeping the group together by encouraging; allowing others to speak; setting standards; accepting others' decisions and expressing group feeling. These latter skills are the most socially oriented, and provide the appropriate circumstances for the more cognitive activities at the top of the list.

Disfunctional behaviours include: being aggressive; arguing or rejecting ideas without consideration; competing to produce the best idea or talk the most; seeking sympathy; messing around; seeking recognition; or withdrawal.

Our data suggests that children seldom opt out of their group's activities; this may be more prevalent at secondary level. But some American researchers (Salomon and Globerson, 1989) have demonstrated that pupils will devise work-avoidance strategies, and they have used the following colourful descriptors to identify possible types of problem: 'free riders', 'suckers' and 'gangers'.

The 'free rider' effect

In certain types of task, especially when performance is dependent on high attaining children (for example, providing ideas for a joint essay), the less able may 'opt out' and simply go through the motions of groupwork without, in fact, making any real input. In other tasks, where a low attaining child is likely to hold back the whole group (for example, when co-operative group reading is slowed down by the poorest reader), it is the high attainers who are most likely to lose motivation, exert little effort and display the free-rider effect. Larger groups allow free-riding more easily than smaller ones.

The 'sucker' effect

Hard-working and motivated group members sometimes come to be less involved if they feel that others are taking advantage of them; that is, they avoid the sucker effect. Thus, children who are enthusiastic and full of ideas may gradually feel that their efforts are no longer worthwhile if others are not also willing to contribute effectively. Non-effective contributions may be judged in terms of both poor performance due to poor ability, or poor performance due to lack of effort.

Ganging up on the task

Children may also find ways round doing the task especially when they see it as pointless or simply do not like the work: 'my partner and I hate writing and we found ways to pretend that we are busy thinking about the essay.' This may also mean that part of the group do all the work on the assumption that: after all, if someone wants to do this task, they are welcome to do so, and if they need more help, then they have to negotiate.

Other effects

If a child's attempted contributions are constantly rejected by the group, then that child is unlikely to continue his effort; alternatively, division of labour may emerge so that each child does only what he is best at or most likes.

In Britain, research on secondary children suggests possible problems with features such as those highlighted above. Other features to watch for are: dominant pupils or those who fail to contribute over a long period of time; conflict in argument which becomes a slanging-match rather than a reflective activity; too much agreement without examining assumptions; problems associating with breaking away from 'habitual' roles, for example, children recognising that a 'class joker' may have a serious contribution, or that a poor reader may be an able problem-solver.

It seems likely that any of these problems will emerge from time to time. If teachers are observant and notice the difficulties, it also seems likely that by making sure that children are aware of and understand the situation, and by talking through the problem with the groups, the majority of issues can be resolved. As one teacher recounts:

> 'When I felt some children were always doing the drawing, or the same children always did the writing, I drew the attention of the group to this and they soon were ensuring everyone tried the full range of activities involved.'

This again highlights how teacher awareness leads to pupil awareness and hence an effective training programme. The teacher's role is obviously central to the whole process of groupwork, especially in terms of making the most of any co-operative activity by being involved in the encouragement of productive behaviours. For this reason, some general features of classroom management and its impact on training are discussed below. This is followed by a section which contains a variety of tasks and activities which can be used to enable children to work co-operatively. Finally, ways in which teachers involve themselves in groups during a collaborative activity in order to further the training process are described.

Management of training tasks

Training needs to take place in a context which allows for the development and reinforcement of social skills. A task recommended by the National Oracy Project (1990) gives children an opportunity to become more aware of group processes by establishing some 'ground rules' for talk, as well as providing a situation in which the teacher can emphasise social behaviour. In groups, pupils are asked to think of between six and ten 'rules' for working together; when these have been decided, the children are asked to make a group poster so that others in the classroom can share these 'rules'. Some examples chosen by a class of top infants were: 'have ideas', 'don't be rude', 'don't be stupid', 'keep trying', 'give information', 'help each other', 'don't keep comments to yourself' and so on.

A teacher could simply give this task to the children in the class and allow them to 'get on with it', hoping that group members would all be fully involved. By circulating around the classroom, it would be possible to pick up any major problems or disagreements. However, it is also possible to plan and structure this activity so that social skills are emphasised, without at the same time telling children what 'ought' to be included on their posters. It is useful at this point to return to the Harlen model (Harlen, 1985) to demonstrate a possible way for setting up this particular task. Although Harlen focusses on teacher and group behaviour in cognitive terms, the same model can be readily adapted in order to emphasise social demands (Figure 7.1).

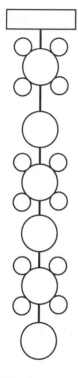

Teacher explains the task – rules for talk/poster. Emphasis on group involvement.

Groups undertake 'brainstorming' exercise for rules and write down ideas. Teacher observes for involvement and may intervene to encourage this, but not to provide ideas.

Groups share rules with rest of class. Teacher ensures that many/all children provide answers to demonstrate involvement. Ways of producing poster discussed. Emphasis on sharing work.

Groups reassemble to design 'rough' posters on rules. Teacher checks for joint participation, encourages this if necessary.

Group posters (rough copy) shared with whole class. Suggestions for improvement made by children.

Group act on suggestions to improve posters, provide top copies. Teacher continues to ensure group involvement.

Soon after – display posters, reference to them; discussion of, for example, how to ensure that 'rules' will be put into action. The teacher will also need to continue emphasising these 'rules' if the children are to realise their importance.

Figure 7.1 Aim: to establish ground rules for talk/involvement of all children

It is quite possible to emphasise co-operative behaviour during any group task. The advantage of the training tasks given in this chapter is that the co-operative focus is explicit. Despite this, the extent to which the teacher stresses, makes clear and monitors the social demand is central to the way in which children will be involved and understand what is required of them.

A teacher of six-year-olds who was involved in our research describes how she set out the ground rules in her own classroom when she first attempted groupwork.

'I felt that it was important to let the children know the **aims** of the task, and that discussion is an important skill. This was in response to, for example, Bennett *et al.* (1984) who criticise teachers for not telling children the aim of a task, and to Cowie and Rudduck (1988) who reports that the children feel "talk" is not "work". I told the children that I wanted to see if they could solve a problem by talking together, and to see if they could help each other work.

There were clear groupwork rules:

  i) **everyone** must join in
 ii) they must help each other
iii) they must not come to me unless there was a problem the group could not solve.

I used role play to emphasise helping (rather than refusing), explaining (rather than giving a simple answer), being polite about asking for help and when receiving help, making eye contact, taking turns and listening to each other.

We discussed the benefits of helpful attitudes and skills such as sitting in a friendly formation, being supportive and the many benefits of working this way which the children and I perceived.

In future I would make it a much more positive policy to encourage and value helping and explaining skills, attitudes and values in my classroom. I would also provide the children with feedback about those gains, so that they perceived the values and benefits of talking and co-operative skills.

When I asked the children why they worked in groups, they said:

− to practice getting on with one another
− to learn things other people know
− to get help with spellings
− to cooperate and help
− to listen to one another
− to think
− to solve problems
− to sort out what you will do.'

The ways of making children aware of groupwork skills are thought to be another central aspect in the development of effective co-operation, and need to be reinforced constantly, whenever children are undertaking groupwork.

Training tasks

A starting point for groupwork recommended by many researchers, and at present being developed by ourselves in an in-service context, is the development of particular kinds of training tasks. Each training activity is deliberately designed to address specific groupwork skills, as well as a range of different purposes for co-operation and different ways in which co-operative efforts can be achieved (whether with a written, drawn or spoken emphasis).

When training children in groupwork skills, it is important that teachers are aware of the kinds of social behaviour encouraged by different kinds of task demand and that the planning of appropriate tasks is central to any training programme. Although training does not mean that the cognitive task requirements become trivialised (and it is often not possible to divorce the cognitive requirements from the social), it *is* possible for teachers to emphasise and focus on one or the other more specifically.

There are three major areas in which task design provides a focal point for training; that is, for tasks which focus specifically on:

(a)   co-operation;
(b)   self-monitoring;
(c)   self-evaluation.

In the first of these, co-operation is central to the task design in that the activity could not be completed without co-ordination between children. For (b) and (c) it might often be possible for the task to be achieved by just one, or any number, of group members, but the focus is on how, and how well, the group operate as a whole. There is a certain amount of overlap between self-monitoring and self-evaluation, although the former tends to be related to monitoring *during* an activity and the latter refers to processes which occur *after* the task, demanding that children reflect on features of the task demand. Examples of each of these three kinds of activity are given below.

The tasks can take many forms, and are often similar to the kinds of 'tight' activity recommended by Biott (1984) (see Chapter 4) for which there is a clear demand both cognitively and socially; for example, the completion of a Cloze exercise. At the secondary level, Cowie and Ruddock (1988) use the word 'techniques' for similar tasks which are designed as a starting point to promote interaction or to get 'ideas flowing'. Such activities:

'clearly embody the key characteristics of groupwork in that they bring small groups together to pool ideas in a framework which positively encourages people to interact and to be creative or to take risks with ideas. However, they are limited and are not, in our view, a substitute for the sustained interaction and depth of understanding that co-operative groupwork supports.'

Jenkin (1989) has provided a workbook of materials for teachers interested in 'making small groups work', and although these also are intended for lower secondary pupils, many of the ideas can be used or adapted for young children. Although Jenkin does not use the word 'training', the tasks are clearly for this purpose, encouraging the building of co-operation and awareness of groupwork skills.

However, it is the American, Kagan, who has done the most work in the area of training primary children in specific groupwork skills (Kagan, 1988). He focusses particularly on the social aspects of activities and he describes how it is possible to 'restructure' tasks so that 'acquisition of social skills is an integral part of the learning experience, or necessary for task completion.'

Kagan gives practical examples of how tasks can be restructured for this purpose, as well as many examples of tasks with inbuilt co-operative activity, and we include some of his ideas in this chapter, as well as turning to Cohen, Jenkin and others for further examples. The purpose of outlining a series of tasks in this chapter is to highlight the different features incorporated within the talk demand of each activity and thus to provide a core of materials which can be purposefully used, adapted or extended by classroom teachers. The chosen tasks have been summarised or adapted from the original versions; many will not be dissimilar from normal classroom activities, but the emphasis will always be on co-operative skills.

Training tasks which demand co-operation

Each of the seven examples of co-operative tasks below contains a specific element which obliges children to work together in order to satisfy the task demand.

(a) **Example 1:** A group mural (Kagan, 1988). Kagan suggests that, in normal circumstances, a group mural may not necessarily promote co-operative group activity. If there is little or no restructuring to emphasise co-operation, then children will tend to work on different areas of the mural, with little interaction or co-operation. However, if certain constraints are imposed, then co-operation will become essential. For this task, each child might be allowed only to use *one* colour crayon (or paint). To be successful, the group must then plan and take decisions as to how their activities can be co-ordinated.

(b) **Example 2:** A group report about 'fun vacation activities' (Kagan, 1988). In a traditional activity of this kind, each child would tend to write about their own vacation. However, if the structure demands that each pupil writes about the 'fun activities' of someone else in the group, rather than their own, this restructuring will ensure that interviewing skills are developed.

(c) **Example 3:** Draw what I like (Kagan, 1988). Working alone, each pupil draws a simple picture (for example, a robot made of eight figures, using only circles, squares and triangles). They then each write a description of their own picture. Working in pairs, children must then attempt to draw each other's pictures by listening to the written description. If the description is inadequate, the pair must work together to edit it. Pairs within the group then exchange the edited samples and attempt the drawing again. If the second attempt is more successful, then the children will have demonstrated for themselves the power of editing.

(d) **Example 4:** Ranking (adapted for the primary age-range from Jenkin (1989)). In a group of four, each pair of pupils is given the same list of nine items, for example – statements, ideas, objects or quotations. Each item, idea, etc, should be written on a separate piece of card. The pairs then rank these ideas into the diamond shape specified in Figure 7.2. A question should be used to form the ranking process; for example – which animal is the most dangerous: tiger, ant, rattle-snake, gorilla, alligator, dog, camel, whale, octopus?

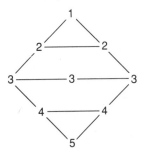

Figure 7.2 A system for ranking

The 1s and 2s of the diamond are the most dangerous/important/urgent/interesting, and so on, the 4s and 5s the least and the 3s in the middle.

Each pair then explains their choices to the other pair in the group of four and the diamond can be arranged by agreement.

(e) **Example 5**: Broken circles (devised by Ted and Nancy Graves; see Cohen (1986)). Cohen recommends a task which emphasises co-operation even more strongly than the previous four activities since it depends entirely on group members *giving* what is necessary to someone else, without the medium of language.

Each person is given an envelope with different pieces of circles. The goal is for each person to put together a complete circle. In order for this goal to be reached, there must be some exchange of pieces. Players are not allowed to talk or take pieces from someone else's envelope; they may not point or signal with their hands. Each player must put together their own circle and may only give pieces. Other group members can accept the pieces given to them if they are appropriate.

There are three versions of the broken circles game, each increasing in difficulty from 'simplest' to 'advanced'. Simple broken circles is suitable for eight- to ten-year-olds in groups of four, and using four envelopes marked W, X, Y, Z. The pattern is given in Figure 7.3. The top line of circles indicates one possible solution to the puzzle. Alternative solutions are shown underneath. Groups that finish quickly can be asked, 'How many other ways of forming four circles can you discover?'

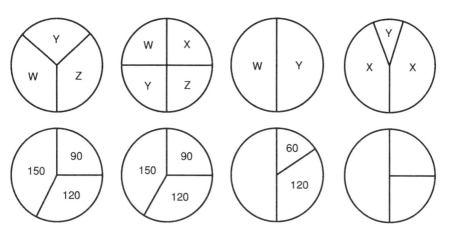

Figure 7.3 Simple broken circles

The five tasks outlined above demand that children work together in order to complete the activity satisfactorily. None of them leaves the need for co-operation to chance in the way that any general request to 'co-operate' might, and this is the major purpose of their use. These tasks allow 'teambuilding' to be emphasised; social skills can be stressed because it is clear to children what kinds of behaviour are being asked of them. This kind of task structuring may be appropriate for many classroom activities, even when children are well used to working together, but at later stages it might be that co-operation could be assumed rather than made the focus of attention.

The next task is devised so that children can become more aware of their own levels of spoken participation within a group.

(f) Example 6: Talking chips (Kagan, 1988). The teacher must choose a simple discussion topic for the pupils. When a child wants to contribute to the talk, a chip (for example, a pen or pencil) must be laid in the centre of the table. That child cannot talk again until all the group's chips have been placed. The chips are then retrieved, and anyone can start the process again.

There are several variations to this process, for example:

- **Timed turns**: no-one can talk for more than a minute and there is a timekeeper on each team.
- **Freebees**: you can briefly respond to yes/no questions without giving up a chip.

Kagan states: 'After using the approach for some time, students internalize the principles of universal and equal participation. Appropriate turn-taking is clearly central to organised discussion, and it does seem that when children are made aware of this and practise it, they really do begin to participate more equally.' Some examples of this kind of development are given in the section on 'teacher intervention' later in this chapter.

The kind of discussion which could be used for the 'talking chips' activity is also one suggested by Kagan; that is, the use of a dilemma situation which, if not actually experienced by the children, is certainly familiar to them.

(g) Example 7: Dilemma situations (Kagan, 1988). Pupils need to 'think themselves' into a situation in order to find a solution. (Similar dilemmas have already been discussed in Chapter 4 under 'task design'.) Kagan provides some examples.

1. Susan and Jane were walking to school. Susan was playing along the way and wasting time. Jane knew if she waited for Susan, she would be late. What should Jane do?
2. During painting time the teacher asked the children to be careful with the paint. Bill accidentally spilled the red paint just as the recess bell rang. What should Bill do?

3. Jennifer borrowed some crayons from her friend Stacy. Jennifer accidentally broke one of the crayons. What should Jennifer do?
4. Bill grabbed the ball away from John during recess. What should John do?'

Discussion of dilemmas is not an activity which in itself demands co-operation, though clearly this would be appropriate; however, in the context of 'talking chips' the co-operative demand becomes the focus of the task.

Those researchers who have been involved in the development of general-purpose training tasks have also contributed ideas for both self-monitoring and self-evaluation activities. A few examples are outlined below.

Activities to promote self-monitoring skills

In the 'talking chips' activity there is a demand that children take turns on a regular basis in their discussion. Through this turn-taking process, pupils are encouraged to pay particular attention to their own behaviour, and this could be seen as the first stage of a self-monitoring process. It is also possible to enable pupils to observe their patterns of verbal contribution in groupwork when they are participating in free-running discussion.

(a) **Example 1**: Observing patterns of verbal contributions (adapted from Jenkin (1989)). Jenkin recommends that this activity be organised by the pupils themselves, one member of the group being chosen to assess patterns of interaction amongst the rest of the group. At the lower primary level, it might be considered less appropriate for children to manage this kind of evaluation for themselves, though with practice most of the older range should be able to cope and to make sense of the patterns. The only problem with removing any one group member in order to observe is that patterns of interaction will inevitably be changed, though for any pupil observer it is likely to be an interesting experience. Over time, all children should be given a chance to observe.

This activity is also a useful technique for any teacher who wishes to evaluate interaction patterns; findings can be fed back to the group so that all, in turn, become more aware of their own contributions.

A small amount of preparation is needed:

1 Circles should be drawn on a large piece of paper and named for each group member, with an additional circle to represent

the whole group. No two circles should be directly opposite each other (Figure 7.4).

2   A line is drawn by the observer between the speaker and the person who is addressed, each time a significant contribution is made. The line ends in an arrowhead at the circle of the person addressed. This person may be addressed by name or may be deduced by non-verbal communication.

3   When a contribution is made to the group in general, a line is drawn from the speaker to the 'group' circle; there is no need for an arrowhead.

A final picture at the end of a discussion (taken direct from Jenkin) could look like that in Figure 7.5.

Another way to focus attention on participation in groupwork is through role development. Initial ideas for this were according to Kagan (1983), and developed by Johnson and Johnson (1985), who assigned key roles to each group member.

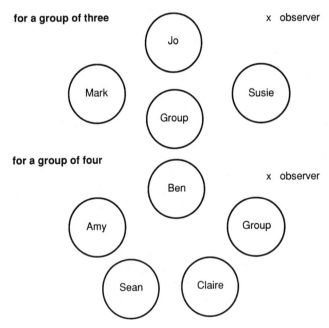

Figure 7.4 A plan for observation of groups

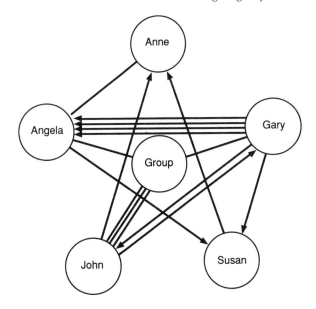

Figure 7.5 A completed observation plan

(b) **Example 2**: Key roles. In a group of four, an individual could be assigned one of the following roles:

- **co-ordinator**: to keep the group on task, to ensure contributions from all, to guide discussion or activity
- **data gatherer**: to take notes or summarise ideas, to clarify ideas and to read aloud from some materials when appropriate
- **secretary**: to record group answers or materials; spokesperson in reporting to the class
- **evaluator**: to keep notes on the group process – how well individuals in the group are working together; to lead any evaluation at the end of the session.

Not only are individuals assigned specific roles, they are taught to analyse the various productive and non-productive roles members play and to work on their own group process.

Providing self-monitoring skills for younger children may provide more of a challenge but the use of pictures to identify key roles, and to aid their thinking, have proved useful, and are reproduced in Figure 7.6 (Kagan, 1988).

KEY ROLES

Captain Sure

CHECKER

Captain Write

WRITER

Captain Quiet

Captain Quiet

Captain Share

Teller

Figure 7.6 Key roles for monitoring of group processes

Cohen recommends another task which has inbuilt monitoring of group processes, but is also dependent on evaluation, thereby achieving a dual purpose.

(c) **Example 3**: Four-stage rocket (amended from Epstein (1972)). The class – divided into groups – are given a short discussion task. The teacher circulates during this, listens, observes and takes notes of good and bad discussion techniques. Next she leads a whole-class feedback session making use of these observations. The children are then told that they will practise four skills necessary for discussion to 'take off like a rocket'. Each is tackled in turn.

1 **Conciseness** – 'getting quickly to the point and not beating around the bush.' A timekeeper is used to watch the clock and ensure that no-one speaks for more than 15 seconds.
2 **Listening** – 'paying attention to what is said.' A different time-

keeper is used to ensure that a participant speaks for no longer than 15 seconds. This time, the next speaker must wait for three seconds before restarting the conversation.

3 **Reflecting** – 'repeating out loud to the group something of what the person before you has said.' With a new timekeeper, adhere to the previous rules; in addition, each new speaker must repeat something just said and this must be accepted by a nod from the previous speaker. Only when a statement has been correctly reflected should the topic be continued.

4 **Everyone contributes** – 'all the people in the group have to speak.' A new timekeeper is selected; all previous rules apply with the addition of one feature – no-one may speak a second time until everyone else has done so.

Each stage demands that pupils constantly monitor their behaviour and input. In addition, each stage needs to be evaluated immediately after taking place and the timekeepers should be able to provide useful feedback to the rest of the class on how their own groups operated and what created the most difficulties. The teachers should make sure that children are clear about why each skill is important.

When all four stages have been completed, there should be a further group discussion without a timekeeper to enforce the rules, but where conciseness, listening, reflecting and contributions from everyone remain central to the task. A pupil observer from each group may be used to report back on the extent that peers do adhere to these skills, and the teacher should listen to and observe differences between the 'pre-rocket' discussion and this latter one. All observations then need to be discussed by the whole class.

Cohen warns that discussion tasks can often finish surprisingly quickly – but suggests a stimulus such as the problem outlined below, which is readily tackled by older primary pupils and cannot be solved instantly, and therefore lends itself to several of the 'rocket' stages. It presents an advanced 'dilemma situation.'

Alligator River

Once there was a girl named Abigail who was in love with a boy named Gregory. Gregory had an unfortunate accident and broke his glasses. Abigail, being a true friend, volunteered to take them to be repaired. But the repair shop was across the river, and during a flash flood the bridge was washed away. Poor Gregory could see nothing without his glasses, so Abigail was desperate to get across the river to the repair shop. While she was standing forlornly on the bank of the river, clutching the broken glasses in her hands, a boy named Sinbad glided by in a rowboat.

She asked Sinbad if he would take her across. He agreed to on the condition that while she was having the glasses repaired, she would go to a nearby store and steal a transistor radio that he had been wanting. Abigail refused to do this and went to see a friend named Ivan who had a boat.

When Abigail told Ivan her problem, he said he was too busy to help her out and didn't want to be involved. Abigail, feeling that she had no other choice, returned to Sinbad and told him she would agree to his plan.

When Abigail returned the repaired glasses to Gregory, she told him what she had had to do. Gregory was so mad at what she had done he told her that he never wanted to see her again.

Abigail, upset, turned to Slug with her tale of woe. Slug was so sorry for Abigail that he promised her he would get even with Gregory. They went to the school playground where Gregory was playing ball and Abigail watched happily while Slug beat Gregory up and broke his glasses.

Rank these characters from "best" to "worst": Abigail, Gregory, Sinbad, Ivan, Slug. Give reasons for your decisions.'

(Simon, Howe and Kirschenbaum, 1972)

A similar activity to this is found in Jelfs (1982): which four out of sixteen items would you collect from your flooding house – for example, your address book, a beautifully bound 1887 atlas which you have borrowed from a friend, a photograph album of the first three years of your life, a long poem which you have been working on for several months and which is at last ready to hand in to the school Poetry Society for the annual magazine, and so on. These ideas can be adapted and extended for pupils of any age-range, and similar dilemmas are easily invented.

Activities to promote self-evaluation skills

Self-evaluation activities are as important as any other aspect of groupwork, for it is through self-evaluation that understanding about success and failure can be gained and from which decisions for improvement can be made. Self-evaluation, by raising awareness after a task, should in turn enable children to be more effective at monitoring their co-operative behaviours during a future activity.

Kagan (1988) also emphasises evaluation processes:

'It is extremely valuable to have students take a good look at their own group process – with an eye toward improving it so that they might each better their goals. As students realise they are tripping over their own process, if they are given time and a structure in which to observe, process and work on improving their functioning, they will. Students in cooperative groups are motivated to improve their group process because improvement helps them reach their goals.'

Children of different ages will clearly need different kinds of evaluation activities; many of those suggested by Kagan take the form of sheets of questions which can be adapted for the particular age-range of the children. He also points out that the evaluation process is complex since it needs to take account of four different possibilities:

(a)   groups need to evaluate the whole group's process.
(b)   group members may be called on to evaluate each other's behaviours and contributions.
(c)   individuals need to evaluate themselves in the context of the group.
(d)   final presentations or products can be evaluated by other groups and the teacher.

Cohen (1986), too, argues that it is important to evaluate the whole process of a group's activity.

(a) Example 1.
When a task such as the 'four-stage rocket' has been completed, she suggests the following questions as guidelines.

> '*What do you think this game was all about?*
> *How do you feel about what happened in your group today?*
> *What things did you do in your group that helped you to be successful in solving the problem?*
> *What things did you do that made it better?*
> *What could the groups do better in the future?*'

She also suggests that the teacher should:

> '*Help participants to be concrete about what they did and also abstract about the general implications of what they did and the lessons they learned for the future.*'

(b) Example 2.
For the youngest children, Kagan suggests a simple pictorial analysis (see Figure 7.7), and the questions may be asked of the whole group together or to individuals.

Figure 7.7 A simple method for evaluating group processes with young children

Group evaluation	Always	Sometimes	Never
1 We checked to make sure everyone understood what we did	.....	.....	.....
2 We answered any questions that were asked	.....	.....	.....
3 We gave explanations wherever we could	.....	.....	.....
4 We asked specific questions about what we didn't understand	.....	.....	.....
5 Anyone who had difficulty got extra practice and help	.....	.....	.....
6 We paraphrased what others said to be sure we understood	.....	.....	.....

Group signatures

X ....   X ....

X ....   X ....

Figure 7.8 Evaluation of group processes

(c) **Example 3.**

Lee *et al.* (1985) suggest a group evaluation sheet of the type shown in Figure 7.8.

(d) **Example 4.**

Kagan (1988) also advocates the use of a longer set of questions to which pupils would be expected to turn on many occasions (see Figure 7.9). He suggests that the first three questions would be tackled as

---

1 What one word would you use to describe how the group was today?
....

2 What one word would describe the way you would like the group to be?
....

3 Is everyone participating?
Yes, always .... Usually .... Occasionally ....
Rarely .... No, never ....

4 Are you (everyone in group) trying to make each other feel good? If not, what are you doing?
Yes, always .... Usually .... Occasionally ....
Rarely .... No, never ....

5 Are you trying to help each other feel able to talk and say what you think?
Yes, always .... Usually .... Occasionally ....
Rarely .... No, never ....

6 Are you listening to each other?
Yes, always .... Usually .... Occasionally ....
Rarely .... No, never ....

7 Are you showing you are listening by nodding at each other?
Yes, always .... Usually .... Occasionally ....
Rarely .... No, never ....

8 Are you saying 'That's good' to each other when you like something?
Yes, always .... Usually .... Occasionally ....
Rarely .... No, never ....

9 Are you asking each other questions?
Yes, always .... Usually .... Occasionally ....
Rarely .... No, never ....

10 Are you listening and really trying to answer these questions?
Yes, always .... Usually .... Occasionally ....
Rarely ....

11 Are you paying attention to each other?
Yes, always .... Usually .... Occasionally ....
Rarely ....

12 Is any one person talking most of the time? Yes .... No ....

13 Is there a way to have a group where everyone talks about equally?

Figure 7.9 Evaluation of group processes

often as groupwork occurs and the others enable children to focus on specific issues from time to time. Each question could be used for individual evaluation of the whole group or as a joint activity. What these questions serve to do is to make clear those features of groupwork that Kagan himself believes to be important and to demonstrate to pupils the kinds of social behaviours that are highly valued by the teacher.

Some American researchers (Lee *et al.*, 1985) also tackle evaluation in a different way, by organising teacher-controlled lessons in which children are asked to evaluate their own behaviours alongside the rest of the class.

(e) Example 5.
A sample lesson of this technique is given below.

Strategy : Discussion
Level   : Elementary (Primary)

Step 1: Select an activity
Discussion by the students of how they are working together in their small groups. Students give verbal examples of what they say to encourage others, explain content, resolve conflicts, check for understanding, for help, etc.

Step 2: Make decisions
a Group size: entire class
b Room arrangement: children sitting together in a large circle
c Time allotment: 15–20-minute period spread throughout the year
d Materials needed: chart paper, marker for recording examples.

Step 3: Set the lesson
a Task statement:

'Using the experiences you have had working in small groups, we will discuss how effective your groups have been and what we can do to help all the groups learn more effectively.' (The class will either resolve any problem brought up or focus on a specific group skill or helping behaviour that seems to be lacking.)

b Goal statement:

'This will be a chance for you to use every member of the class as a resource. Think what you can contribute to help others work well in groups or problems you would like help in resolving.'

1 **Means of creating positive interdependence:**
   One chart on which to record ideas

2 **Behaviours expected from children:**

Listening	Looks like:	eye contact, leaning toward speaker
	Sounds like:	'Are you saying ...', 'I'd like to add ... to what ... said.'
Contributing ideas	Looks like:	eye contact with the group
	Sounds like:	'One idea is ...', 'You might try...' 'You could say ...'

c Criteria for success:

The chart will be filled with possible alternatives to develop a skill or resolve a problem.

Step 4: Monitor and process
a The discussion is in itself a monitoring process.
b The teacher will monitor the discussion and give feedback on how many are contributing, who is making eye contact, etc.

Step 5: Anticipate possible problems and interventions
a Possible problems:
   1 Some children may not contribute
   2 Some children may not listen
b Possible interventions:
   1 Encourage those who have not contributed to share ideas, elaborate ideas, say how you think an idea would work in his/her group, etc;
   2 Ask some children who haven't been listening to paraphrase ideas, say how they think an idea could apply to their group.

By working in this way, the teacher sensitises children to important skills in working together. The evaluation process should in turn enable the pupils to be more effective at both monitoring and evaluating their own groupwork activities.

Teacher involvement in groups during training

Teachers report that they often work with and alongside groups during the training programme, intervening in many different ways, but always with the same purpose – to enable children to interact more effectively and with greater sensitivity towards each other. By making children more aware of the ways in which they behave and the ways in which they might adapt their behaviour for more effective co-operation, teachers are likely, over a period of time, to enable pupils to self-monitor and self-evaluate more fruitfully.

Several of the teachers working with us planned out courses of training with specific targets for each groupwork session. Some of these lessons are described below. Although most involve very young children, the kinds of interaction and the purposes will be similar across the primary age-range.

As part of a topic on movement, a class of infants paid a visit to their local swing park. The opportunity was used to reinforce classroom work on shapes and angles as well to consider the different movements of the playground apparatus. After a class discussion on the poor facilities of their own park in comparison to others known by the children, and on what they would like to see in an ideal park, the children divided into groups of four to plan and then build their own swing parks.

During the building stage, the teacher noticed that Michael was somewhat of an outsider in his group and decided to intervene by asking how he was going to make the planned football pitch. Although Simon immediately answered the teacher's question, Owen reacted with more sensitivity and made his own effort to draw Michael in to help with the making of a climbing net. Simon then responded in a similar way, specifically asking Michael to help.

Owen (to Michael:)	We could do knots [talking of climbing net].
Simon:	We could make the base of straws of something. Shall I get the net started?
Michael:	Use a green felt tip to make the pitch [going back to football].
Owen:	If we help each other we can make the net.
Simon:	Michael, will you help me? I can't hold it on my own.
Owen:	I'll cut the string for you.
Simon:	We must get it level.
Owen:	I'm going to cut a hole in it.
Simon:	Righty o – you're the boss.

It seems that it was the teacher intervention that alerted Simon and Owen to Michael's lack of participation, and from this point onwards Michael was invited by the others to work with them. Although he was still not involved in the discussion, he certainly became involved in the action. Thus, even the youngest children can be sensitive in terms of encouraging co-operative activity, and their role in this instance was quite as important as that of the teacher.

A teacher of a reception class sat with a group of four children so that he would be able to encourage them to interact co-operatively. He gave them the following task: pretend to be a removal company taking furniture into the doll family's new house.

The teacher observed and listened until such point as he felt intervention would be useful. These interventions were clearly spontaneous within the context, though the situation was pre-planned, and they never dominated the interaction.

Neil:	Here's the baby's thing [safety gate]
Christina:	Don't put it there Neil, the baby'll fall downstairs.
Cathy:	What does that go on? [the safety gate]
Teacher:	Ask the other children, perhaps they can help you?
Christina:	That's a gate [putting it in front of the front door space].
Teacher:	[to Christina] What would you have a gate there for?
Christina:	If they knock the gate down it means they're trying to get on to the road.
Teacher:	We don't want that, do we.
Neil:	We could put it by the baby's bed in case he falls out.
Christina:	Oh! That's a clever idea.
Cathy:	Push the bed next to the wall.

The children played with the furniture for a while, but seemed unsure where they should put items. After a while, the teacher decided to ask a question to prompt decision-making and further talk.

Teacher:	Have you decided which room is which?
Cathy:	I'll show you – that's the bathroom. That's the bedroom and that's the living room.
Neil:	This is all the bedrooms.
Christina:	That's for the living room, Neil – that doesn't go in here at all.
Peter:	I need some drawers [he picks up the outer casing of a chest of drawers].
Cathy:	Two drawers – here you are.
Christina:	If you've sorted that it goes here.
Cathy:	Ah the baby's cot – that goes in the mummy's bedroom.
Peter:	And the daddy's.
Cathy:	There. I know where that goes [vanity unit]. That's to look in the mirror when you've cleaned your teeth.

The teacher always encouraged group participation, deliberately referring questions back to the group and using simple strategies to extend their thinking. At the same time, the children were clearly aware of each other; for example, Christina's enthusiastic 'Oh! That's a clever idea', or Cathy's instant handing of the drawers to Peter.

Another teacher from our research sample describes how he set up a training situation for nursery children by modelling the kinds of social and cognitive processes that he wanted these young children to emulate. Below he describes some of his feelings about trying groupwork with such young children and the reasons for choosing a specific task – the lotto game. Since this teacher was specifically interested in language development, he discusses problems that he encountered in this area as he gradually realised that his choice of talk had some unexpected limitations.

For the training process, it was important with such young children that the teacher played the game with them until they were thoroughly familiarised with it and until they developed the idea of working as a group together. In terms of language, he took care to elaborate beyond what was necessary simply in terms of playing the game, modelling the kind of interaction that he hoped would later be used by the children when they played the game by themselves.

Teacher: A house that looks like a ship with lots of different roofs. Oh, yes, isn't it beautiful. It's got a ladder to the front door . . . And who's got the white house with the blue windows?

Sophie: Me!

The children were well-prepared by this rehearsal to take on this game by themselves and several groups were organised to play by themselves. The same teacher now describes the ways in which the children participated when he was not present in the group. He deliberately handed over his organising role to one high attaining pupil in each group, asking this child to act as 'group leader'.

In terms of language, the pattern of questioning by each of the pupil leaders was narrow and repetitive; they made no attempt to use any aspect of the teacher's elaborate language. This aspect of the modelling process seemed to have failed.

'Who's got a cow?
Who's got a rocking horse? Kimberley!
Who's got some building bricks?
Who's got this?'

Answers were equally brief; the longest utterances appeared to be associated with progress reports: 'I only got one, two, three, four.' Some players who were usually chatty and had a well-developed use of language, proved to be both limited and narrow in their use of language during the game. The only time that the level of conversation was raised, both in terms of amount and complexity of talk, was during a dispute.

For the children, winning is clearly the point of the game. For one group the final half of the game is taken up by their calling out that they have been beaten (the others), although they continue to claim cards. Yet at the end of the game, Jess clearly announces that they have all won.

Robert: [shouts] Yeah, we beat, we beat.
Jess: Mr Roberts, we all beat.

The kind of language beginning to emerge was different from that when the teacher was present. Further to this, the group leader was certainly tested in a new situation. Indeed, Tania took on the role of the teacher in trying to make the children behave.

Helen: I'm tired, give me a bed please . . .
Tania: No, you're not, no, you're not, cos you've got a . . . cos I'm doing . . . Helen . . . Helen . . . Helen . . . heh! . . . Oh dear, wake up . . .

and then a few seconds later:

Helen: I'm going to bed, everyone.
Patsy: Snack time.
Tania: No we just finish this game . . .
Helen: Oh, I've got that one [referring to the card]
Julie: Finished!
Tania: You'd better be quick, quick, quick.

and at the end:

Tania: Hurry up. Finish up now. Lisa wins.

Interestingly, when Tania says they must 'just finish this game' the children don't all rush off for snack time but *do* finish, demonstrating that they *are* co-operating as a group. In many ways, the narrow task of playing a lotto game in order to win proved to be an effective task in terms of social demand and did allow for important interaction about the social aspects of game playing – for example, completing the game, sorting out misunderstandings, or not being over-concerned about winning. For these reasons, it served its purpose well as a training task for co-operation, at the same time as demonstrating that it was less suitable for encouraging the development of language.

Some teachers plan for different kinds of intervention over a period of time, so that their pupils are constantly reminded of the kinds of skills that are appropriate in groupwork. For example, one teacher describes how she used a whole range of activities to train one particular group as an experiment and before using similar techniques with the rest of the class of seven- to nine-year-olds. The group was chosen from amongst others since the six children seemed to have particular problems if asked to work together.

Some of the training activities are outlined below. For example, when the children had made wave trays, the teacher asked each child to find a sentence to describe to the rest of the group what they had just done. This activity emphasises turn-taking and explanation. Some of their replies were as follows:

Kim: I kept shuffling mine up and down. Mine . . . mine . . . was . . . going each way and they kept hitting each other, all the time.

Steven: I made . . . I made some waves that, they looked like a tartan.

Mark: I made some waves that looked like a chess board. They kept in the middle. They kept colliding with each other.

Serena: I, I, made some waves like Jeremy did, but they hit in the middle.

The children were set a series of groupwork tasks and the teacher observed their involvement closely. She noticed in particular when a child was not participating and intervened with statements such as: 'Steven, tell the group what *you* . . . (think, could do, etc)'. She also requested that the children really listen to each other and respond to statements rather than simply continuing their own train of thoughts, as was frequently the case. Steven and Serena demonstrated that they were well able to build on, challenge, or support each other's ideas when it had been pointed out that this was a useful behaviour:

Serena: Or you could build a glider . . . or hang-glider.
Steven: What out of?
Serena: Out of a tree. Yes, and some material [laughs].

Steven: And where would you get the material? From our clothes?
         [laughter]
Serena: We can make a boat or a raft or something and row over.
Steven: Yes, yes. That's a good idea!

Further to this intervention strategy, the teacher asked that the group evaluate their own behaviours with the use of self-evaluation sheets. By the end of the training period which had been carefully monitored and assessed throughout, the teacher believed that the group had radically changed as a whole and that this was due to different patterns of change for each individual group member. From observations of each of the six children, before, during and after training, she argued that the training process has the potential to:

(a)   modify behaviour (eg, Mark);
(b)   improve degrees of sociability (eg, Steven);
(c)   increase task-related talk (eg, Serena);
(d)   improve motivation, concentration and performance (eg, Jeremy);
(e)   increase involvement (eg, Kim);
(f)   improve confidence in own ability (eg, Roseanne).

As an observation on her own role as teacher, she comments on the importance of intervention in the training process; her own input enabled the children to become aware of their behaviour, encouraged co-operation, and so on, so that the pupils themselves could then use groupwork to their best advantage.

This kind of change is not unique. Another teacher describes two tasks tackled by reception children – one before a period of training and one at the end of it. For the pre-training task, the children were asked to sort a collection of objects and containers into two categories – light or heavy. Their teacher describes how this task was attempted:

'I had to leave the children completely by themselves to avoid every spoken word being addressed to me, rather than to other members of the group. One of the children (the high-achiever) immediately took my place becoming a peer tutor. Unfortunately, she was very bossy and disparaging about the efforts of the other children. I was expecting the low-achiever to be quiet as is his nature, but both of the middle achievers are normally confident and forthcoming. Yet on this occasion, one of them appeared to have been intimidated into virtual silence.'

The following extract of talk clearly demonstrates Emily's dominance:

Emily: No, no. What **are** you doing?
Alex: I've only got one.
Emily: Right. I want to show you something. See this and this?
         Right . . . that one in there, and that one in there . . . that
         one's heavier than that one.
Emily: Take them out again then . . . I said take them out again
         then. Janet, when you've finished weighing them take them
         out again.
Janet: [large sigh]
Emily: And do it all over again.
Alex: This is what I'm doing.
Emily: No, not yet!
Alex: This is what I'm putting in.
Emily: We don't want **everything** in there. What are you doing?

This activity was finally abandoned since the children had forgotten
what it was they were meant to be doing. However, it seems
extraordinary that the group continued with the task at all, given
Emily's attitude to the others; Alex must have been a particularly
tolerant child, persevering with his attempts to work things out himself
and not losing his temper.

After some weeks of training, with the teacher intervening to point
out how the children might work better together on similar tasks, a
post-training activity was given to find out which, from a selection of
objects and containers, would float in a water tray. The children's talk
gives evidence of a great deal of change which persisted throughout
the session. Although Emily spoke most often, she was not dismissive
of the others as before and she allowed the group to work and interact
together. Rather than bossing the others and telling them exactly what
to do, she worked alongside them; the style of her language seems
changed: 'I'm going to see if . . .' Rather than 'Right, I'm going to
show you something.'

Janet: I think this will [float].
Emily: I think this will . . . yes . . . it's floating.
David: This will as well.
Alex: No, it won't.
Emily: Try this one.
Alex: Where do we put this one?
Janet: Put this one on top.
Emily: What if we put this on it? No . . . what if we put this one
         on top and then that one?
Janet: What if we let this one? It's finished . . . look!

All four children were more equally involved than in the pre-training task: they took more equal turns in the conversation, they were all testing out possibilities, they were tentative and questioning and there was use of the word 'we' rather than the constant 'I'; Emily no longer imposed her will in order to dominate the situation.

Their teacher was concerned that there was still not enough co-operation and that they did not always listen or take in what others were saying. However, there can be no doubt that the 'atmosphere' of the group has changed remarkably for the better; in addition, the task was completed. For these pupils in their first year of schooling, it seems likely that a firm foundation for groupwork has been set for the future. It will, however, be important to continue working in this way with these children in order that the groundwork will be of lasting benefit.

Another reception class teacher describes how she used a 'café' as a training area over a long period. A group of four children were monitored over a period of four weeks either playing as a group without adult intervention or role-playing in the presence of an adult (student or teacher). These latter sessions constituted the 'training programme'. The café was set up in one corner of the classroom and the children were free to choose it as an activity area throughout the day. Having had the opportunity to play freely in the café, but before the group had had any contact with an adult in this situation, the children were recorded. The following extracts of talk show that the session was far from successful in terms of co-operation.

Sasha: What would you like?
Penny: Egg on cheese.
Sasha: John, don't kick the table.
Penny: I would like a cup of tea.
John: Nobody take any notice of that.
Simon: An apple, a chip.
Sasha: What would you like?
John: Chips. Eggs. Chips.
Simon: I can't. I'm not playing in here any more.
Sasha: Miss, can you tell John? Chips and eggs . . .
Sasha: Who wants to be cook?
Simon: Uh, huh.
John: I will.
Simon: Me, I will.
Sasha: Oh you won't. Go back to the table.
John: No, I want to be the cook.
Sasha: No you can't.
John: I want to be. I want to be. That's not fair.

Sasha: Well you can't, that's all.
John: [sulks] That's not fair. I want to be.
Simon: No-one wants to.

From this talk, it can be seen that Sasha made an effort to keep the role-play going and briefly gained some positive responses from Penny and John, though John soon started playing around. Unfortunately, both his and Simon's attempts to participate in the group as cook was rebuffed by Sasha, as was a later attempt to 'get the dinner'.

After this, a student teacher in the classroom spent time playing with the children and giving them specific roles in the café: a waitress, a cook and three customers (including herself). She helped the pupils act out their roles and encouraged appropriate language and actions. The class teacher now describes these sessions, as well as explaining how other classroom activities complement this work.

'A typical play session with the student would include:
– deciding who was going to be the cook/the waiter/waitress (stressing turn-taking).
– greeting each other, giving out the menus, looking at the menus, appropriate conversation when ordering, play-writing in the order note book.
– fetching and serving the food.
– eating and drinking.
– paying.

Alongside this there were ongoing activities which were cross-curricular in nature, such as making hot and cold drinks, making jelly, or baking, and then serving or eating the food or drink in the café situation. Children also laid the table, set plates, designed menus, made playdough food to use in the café and used money to pay for food.'

The teacher believed these activities to be an important part of the training programme since they were designed to encourage realistic play and co-operative interaction. She was also involved in specific training sessions with the group, and the ways in which she encouraged the children to participate are shown in the extract of talk below. During this session, Simon (whom she describes as quiet and submissive) was given the role of waiter so that he was obliged to participate more actively.

Teacher: What do we need now?
Simon: Cups.
Sasha: Ssh ... something which starts with a ssh ... What's that ... Saucer. What is it?

Simon:	Saucer.
Sasha:	Good boy. Thank you. What about then we have to have some cups. Right here, right take one at a time. One for John. Well I don't have one so . . . oh thank you.
Teacher:	Thank you Simon.
Penny:	Thank you Simon.
John:	I'm holding it.
Teacher:	Thank you Simon. What do we need now?
John:	Waiter, waiter. Slurp, slurp.
Sasha:	Piggy.
Teacher:	Simon hasn't poured the tea out yet has he? What else do we need?
Sasha:	Spoons, knives, forks.
Teacher:	How many spoons do we need Rebecca?

Nearly four weeks after the initial audio-recording, the teacher again recorded the children's talk. (A few minutes of this session are given below.) The difference in participation is clear; the major problem now seems to be associated with identifying the food! They start by saying 'good morning' to each other and choosing seats.

Sasha:	Do you want a menu?
Penny:	Yes please.
John:	Yeah.
Simon:	I do. I want to see that one with a yoghurt.
Penny:	I do please waitress.
John:	Yes I do.
Penny:	Thank you.
John:	Thank you.
Penny:	Here you are then.
Simon:	Thank you. I want banana yoghurt.
Sasha:	OK . . .
Simon:	I want all these.
Sasha:	Certainly.
John:	I want a pasty too please. What's this? . . .
Sasha:	Just a minute . . .
Penny:	We don't have a cook. What is that?
Sasha:	The cakes.
John:	Who's going to be the cook? You can be the cook, Penny. What is that, waitress?

If this sequence is compared with the first one when the children were unused to the café situation, the changes seem enormous. John, in particular, participated in a completely different way, fully involved and even beginning to organise the others; Sasha no longer dominated, but interacted as an equal; Simon played a full part; Penny showed the least change in her performance but was now supported by the rest of the group. All the children modelled the teacher's politeness in addressing each other.

In the long term, the aim of teacher intervention during training is to enable the groups to be effective enough at monitoring their own activities for an adult presence to be unnecessary. Another aspect of the teacher's role (which can be a stage of the training programme) is making it clear to children that at certain times they must not make any demands on the teacher's time and that their groups must serve as the only source of reference. In the following section, teachers describe the impact of training on this aspect of their classroom management.

Managing pupil demands

A description of changes in pupil demand has already been given in Chapter 3. It was shown that when teachers are positive in their requests for fewer demands and reinforce the importance of the group, they are likely to clear time for themselves. Training children to accept the requirement not to make demands was managed by teachers in different ways.

It is possible to set up a task in such a manner as to make it quite clear to pupils that the teacher is 'not available'. A middle school teacher describes how he set up an activity in an original way – though there is nothing unusual about the task itself – so as to reinforce his exclusion from the event. All necessary materials were provided and laid out before the children entered the room. In order to heighten the motivation level, the teacher used a role-playing device – telling the pupils that they were secret agents going on a mission. The following statement was then read to the class:

> 'You are about to undertake a task. The instructions will be read out to you and the materials needed to help you complete the task are on the table in front of you. I shall remain with you but I cannot help you with the task. Indeed I shall be unable to speak once the task is started and the stop watch set. You may refer to the instruction sheet as many times as you wish. Good luck on your mission. There is a small reward at the end.'

The instruction sheet is reproduced in Figure 7.10. Setting up the task in this way proved to be effective, and the teacher had no demands made on him during this period.

The strength of a specifically designed task such as this is that the demand is made clear to the children – their teacher does not want them to come to him for any help. The reasons for pupils demanding attention from the teacher are many and various; they may be necessary or important, but they may also be due to poor planning and management, and to lack of explicit instruction as to the kinds of behaviour that are appropriate. Demands may also be created when the task instructions or content are poorly presented or are unsuitable for the ages or ability of the pupils.

However, when children are explicitly told, for example, that they must ask for help from their group before coming to the teacher, they seem prepared to accept this. The habit will need to be acquired and reinforced over time, which is why it must be clearly linked to an overall training process. Reason, Rooney and Roffe (1987) also emphasise:

'Teachers can enhance cooperation by actively encouraging young children to work together and help each other. By doing so they not only promote social development but increase teacher time for individual work.'

Making a bridge

You have been selected as a group to work together to construct a bridge.

The finished bridge must be approximately 30 cm in length and be able to support a weight of 500 g.

Unfortunately the only materials available are:

- two newspapers
- a roll of sellotape
- a pair of scissors

- a ruler
- a 500 g weight
- a stop watch.

and your collective brainpower!

The success of this mission will depend upon your ability to talk the problem through and to work together.

Remember, 'a problem shared is a problem halved.'

The time limit for this task is 30 minutes.

Figure 7.10 Instruction sheet for a group task

Kagan suggests that old habits die hard, and he describes one way in which teacher demand can be changed by providing a rule which makes team responsibility all important.

> 'When first assigned to teams, students will raise their hands and expect individual attention. They thus force the class back into a whole-class structure with only one student at a time participating. A neat way out of this is to have a rule: team questions only. If a student has a question he or she must try first to get it answered within the team. If no one on the team knows the answer, the team can consult with another team. If both do not know, then four hands rather than one go up, signalling need to consult with the teacher.'

Several teachers from our own research also describe how they used similar kinds of method to encourage group independence.

> 'The idea of moving from individual work to group outcomes required, as a first stage, children to work cooperatively in classroom management. They were encouraged to provide the answers to their own problems, only seeking the teacher's help when they could not provide an answer as a group. I needed to explain and remind them before each session of the rules. Sometimes they would forget and just come straight to me, but generally they picked up the rules of the new game quickly. It is perhaps worth noting that the "conditioned dependency" which some teachers tend to consider as good, caring teaching was hard to break. Many children were seeking reassurance from an adult rather than genuine help from the teacher.'

This teacher was willing to answer questions relating to cognitive difficulties within the task, but part of his training programme centred on refusing to be involved in other kinds of demand – for example, sorting out materials or 'behaviour niggles'.

As previously described, the allocation of roles to group members can be used as a method of reinforcing group responsibility. One teacher set up a formal period of training, using narrow language exercises and always ensuring that there was a group leader to turn to in case of difficulty. Although in the long run she seldom requested that groups should be entirely self-sufficient, she did find that children could give and ask each other for help without disrupting the group's conversation and that she herself became more relaxed, knowing that pupils were conscientious in the ways they worked together.

Through training, teachers are developing what are often known as metacognitive skills in children – that is, skills which enable them to be good learners. In terms of groupwork, pupils may come to realise that they *are* able to make decisions for themselves rather than depending on the teacher, they may learn to what extent they can rely on others, they may find strategies for sorting out their own difficulties. Such features will enable individuals, over time, to become more autonomous in their learning.

Many teachers commented on how their training of pupils was essential to the development of independent learning, but were also surprised at the speed with which children did become responsible for both their own work and that of the group. One teacher states:

'Having established a collaborative way of working the children were obviously far less reliant on me. Demands made on me dropped significantly, thus enabling me to provide appropriate backup where necessary. Confidence had transferred to the group and they had all the tools to work independently. Before grouping the children obviously relied heavily on me for evaluation and direction in what to do next but, on the implementation of co-operative groups, they evaluated each other's work within the group.'

Another teacher says:

'The children who have now been working with me for almost a year have adapted well to the idea of co-operation and asking other children for help. Those children who have joined the class this term (due to class reorganisation) have found this practice more difficult and are still quite demanding of my attention. However, I feel that overall the majority of the children are thinking more for themselves, are using each other for help when they need it and are becoming more independent.'

Kerry and Sands (1982) suggest that, 'In groupwork the children themselves are personally much more involved in the work than they may be in a traditional class lesson, and the teacher may even feel redundant.' This was a feeling shared by several of the teachers involved in our research. Yet the feeling of redundancy soon changed as it became clear that the time made available could be used to advantage in different ways – for the kinds of monitoring or assessment discussed in Chapter 8.

Summary

As with the whole teaching and learning process, the training process can be seen as cyclical in nature. First of all, teachers need to set up a training, or awareness-raising, programme. This may be done through the provision of simple tasks to emphasise co-operative ways of working, and may be largely organised and managed by the teacher. Further tasks should allow teachers to continue raising children's awareness about effective co-operation and social skills, either by monitoring and being involved in groups during co-operative tasks, or through evaluation at the end of a groupwork session, perhaps with individual groups but also with the whole class being involved in feedback and discussion.

At the same time as the teacher encourages, develops and evaluates co-operation, there is a need for the children to be given tasks which enable them to monitor and evaluate their own behaviour in groups and become responsible for their own group's performance. Thus both teacher and pupils need to participate in monitoring and evaluation, which will in turn have an impact on future co-operative activities.

The teacher's role in this training process can be summarised in diagrammatic form as in Figure 7.11. Thus, children can be enabled to work more effectively in groups by making them aware of appropriate behaviours; teachers must then observe the process of groupwork in order to diagnose any problems either with learning or with the social relationships of the group; these observations and general evaluation must then be fed back to the pupils to enable them to be more sensitive about the ways in which they work together. Pupils are then enabled to be more effective in monitoring their own activities in future tasks. The cycle starts again when the information gained by the teacher during this process is used to inform training activities. A similar cycle applies equally well to cognitive processes, and this is outlined in Chapter 9.

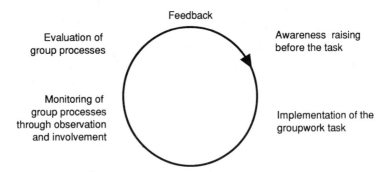

Figure 7.11 A cycle of training in groupwork

8 Assessing groupwork

The assessment of groupwork falls into two major categories; some kinds of assessment will take place *during* a groupwork task, but many other assessments can be made *after* a task has been completed.

Monitoring groupwork processes is obviously an activity that must take place while children are working together. This will usually be achieved through observation, either informally across the class or with a single group, or formally for assessment purposes, with check-lists relating to the statements of attainment. It is also possible to monitor group processes after the event by listening to audio (or watching video) recordings of a group at work. Both direct observation and evidence from audio recordings are discussed below. Different modes of assessment are then outlined.

Observation

Observation of groups can be for different purposes, but the basic dichotomy between social and cognitive processes remains central. Observation must relate to features such as diagnosis of error and to monitoring many of the specific cognitive demands of the National Curriculum; it must also, as stated in the SEAC *Source Book of Teacher Assessment* (SEAC, 1990), relate to assessment of social demands – how well children work together in terms of sharing tasks, sharing involvement, participating in task-related talk and activities, and so on.

The SEAC guidelines state not only that 'Group work requires the teacher to decide how best to manage and observe what is taking place,' but also that:

'Observation of process has to be planned for. Such observation for assessment should be analytical, moving beyond a general impression, into seeing what the child is actually doing. By being systematic in approach, familiarity with Statements of Attainment will increase.'

Teachers will clearly have to make decisions about, for example, whether observation is for the purpose of assessing attainment of individuals within the group, and whether the focus will be on cognitive or social aspects of the task. This instantly becomes problematical, since a narrow and clear focus allows for more specific observation, and yet the processes of groupwork tend to be so complex and overlapping that they cannot necessarily be separated out. The relationships between the cognitive and social demands of a task, and individual and group participation may be so intricately interwoven that observation of separate features is not possible.

The SEAC report contains a case study which illustrates the kinds of difficulty.

'As the group planned and carried out the presentation [an oral report on a visit to the airport], the teacher observed them and recorded her observations on a check-list which included the features which had previously been identified as indicating attainment.

From the teacher's observations, it became clear that one member of the group dominated both the planning and presenting, whilst another remained passive, contributing little to the group discussion during planning and being content to participate as directed by the others.

The teacher expressed concern about her observations for these two individual children, because in designing the check-list such issues had not been taken into account.'

The source book's response to such a situation does not really serve to clarify the problematic nature of observation, whether formal or informal. It merely states:

'This example demonstrates the need for a clear focus on the task, its demands and its relation to the criteria for assessment. Whilst assessment tasks should be clearly planned and structured it is necessary that teachers are adaptable in order to respond to pupil performance and behaviour which is not anticipated.'

A statement such as this is not necessarily helpful to teachers since it does not demonstrate how such features can be achieved. In addition, in the particular instance outlined above, the children, whatever their participation or personality, had 'planned and participated in a presentation', as demanded by the Statement of Attainment. In a narrow sense, all children may have satisfied the attainment criteria, and yet the teacher clearly felt that two pupils in particular were lacking in interpersonal skills.

Throughout this book we have provided details of children's responses to tasks as well as the kinds of skills that are practised in training programmes. These details should enable teachers to anticipate some of the ways in which pupils may work and talk in groups, and how children can operate together when circumstances permit. This should in turn, allow teachers to be more deliberate in their planning for assessment; yet the task will inevitably remain difficult.

The teachers with whom we have worked do observe regularly and carefully, especially since learning to manage the demands on their time more carefully. This again is a point raised by SEAC:

'Assessing pupils by observing them takes attention and concentration. This can be reduced by interruptions; however, if a teacher ignores an interruption or sends away a child with a query, this could signal that assessment is not part of normal classroom life, yet is somehow more important. This may be unhelpful.

It may be better to think in terms of 'red activities', those requiring on-the-spot observation, and 'green activities', those where the products can be looked at afterwards.

In planning these activities, it helps to think about the distribution of activity in the classroom.'

There are many ways in which classroom management can be used to emphasise the 'normality' of assessment and to make sure that those pupils not being assessed do not feel neglected. However, one of the most appropriate ways to achieve this is by the use of co-operative groupwork, when children are more dependent on their group than on their teacher. They soon become used to a routine wherein, for some parts of the week, it is made clear that group responsibility is all-important.

SEAC also raises the issue of 'copying' — 'where one member of a collaborative group uses the contribution of another inappropriately' (4.11); however, in the kinds of problem-solving activity advocated throughout this book, 'copying' is unlikely to feature since the purpose of tasks is that ideas, ways of working, and so on, need to be shared and group decision-making is important. 'Copying' only becomes an issue when individual products are the sole emphasis.

Several of the teachers involved in our research found that by clearing time they were able to assess some aspects of groupwork. One suggests that he was able to observe a group of pupils in order to assess:

'– their ability to co-operate
– their understanding of the task and of how to implement its completion
– the suitability of the task in meeting their needs
– how the working group gels and how best its composition may be altered when necessary
– who is helping whom in each group and if the help is aiding the understanding of the task
– how suitable the resources available to learners are and how effectively the resources are used.'

Yet he also admits that the complexity of classroom processes is such that it is extremely difficult to come to hard-and-fast conclusions about group relationships or learning.

The teachers in our study tended to focus most easily on social behaviours. This may be because such behaviours are most available for observation, whereas evidence of cognitive activity or progress may not always be observable from instant to instant, but may need retrospective analysis in the context of a completed task. The following description demonstrates how a teacher picked up social problems through observation.

'Sometimes a pupil may decide they cannot be bothered to work through things with a group. One of our pupils this year frequently showed that she wanted to get on with things in her own way. She made no fuss and did all the work necessary, sometimes doing everyone else's as well so that it could be done her way. As she was quietly industrious and as the other members in the group were happy to let her do it, this was not obvious unless we carefully watched the groups as they worked . . . Another boy opted out of his group accusing the others of not listening to him. I discussed both of these problems with the whole class to try to make the children realise that each of them had something to offer, that they should value each other and be able to feel a valued member of a group themselves.'

The links with training again become apparent at this point. If teachers are aware of the kinds of social behaviours that are appropriate for co-operative work, and if they act upon their observations of failure to participate appropriately, then they continue to reinforce the training programme. Thus observation is not only important for assessment criteria, but also for the betterment of group processes.

Audio recordings

Observation of groups is clearly important as part of the monitoring process, but observation alone is not always adequate. Teachers who have been involved in the audio taping of groupwork are the first to admit this, since listening closely to pupils allows for different kinds of judgement: 'It is not always possible to observe a group closely, and I would have judged far more of the talk to be off-task than it actually was.'

Biott (1984) learned from his project that evaluation of children by analysing tapes of their task provided some surprises. He quotes a teacher from another project who, having listened to tapes of group talk, said 'it can be like being "witness to mental activity in the raw."'(Lunzer and Gardner, 1979).

He states that:

'Whilst the teacher's attention is mainly focussed on the unit of the whole group, its understanding and its corporate progress, views about individual pupils are inevitably being developed. However, after having recorded, transcribed and analysed pupil interaction in groups the teachers involved in the project were more cautious about the way they were making judgements about their pupils' ability and progress . . . Ad hoc observation may be misleading. For instance, the pupil who seems to assume the role of leader at the outset by, say, reading out the instructions or taking control of materials does not necessarily contribute more to the quality of the co-operation during the activity. Furthermore, some pupils might show evidence of skills which have not been apparent when the teacher is there. It is important that we acknowledge the provisionality of any picture we build up of our pupils. Misleading impressions can also be gained by the teacher who moves around the groups, asking questions, listening and talking to pupils. In one example, a teacher asked a group how they were getting on and was given an account and some ideas by a girl in the group. A recording later revealed that the girl had been given little opportunity to participate by two dominant boys, and the ideas she related to the teacher had not been discussed. The more systematic collection of evidence had thus revealed useful information which more haphazard evaluation had left hidden.'

Biott also gives examples of a girl who usually performs well academically and has a high standard of written work, being negative and inhibitive to reflective and experimental enquiry during groupwork, whereas an apparently less academic child shows marked ability in discussion. She invites comments, has ideas, builds on the ideas of others, exhibits qualities of leadership, and so on. Her true ability became apparent only when her teacher had the opportunity to listen to a taped session.

Teachers involved in our own research reported similar surprises and complexities. Comments such as the following were usual:

> 'I thought that I knew my children well, but I have discovered much more about them as individuals through listening to the tape recordings. In some groups I thought I knew which child might emerge as a leader but in several instances I was mistaken. Some children whom I had previously thought of as timid and easily discouraged proved to be very persistent.'

> 'I had previously thought that girl groups tended to interact well but I found that these groups of girls were quite disagreeable. The boys tended to agree without demur when I had expected much more dissension.'

Such observations allowed teachers to reconsider the ways in which they approached groupwork, since their expectations of individuals had been changed. There were a few instances where teachers were really shocked by their misjudgements; for example, when a girl who seemed to be 'very polite, nicely spoken, keen and helpful' showed herself to be particularly unpleasant when communicating with peers, thus explaining her lack of close friends; or when a reception boy demonstrated such a lack of social skills that his teacher realised that he would need a special programme to help integrate him into classroom activities. In this way, listening to audio recordings allows more sensitive behaviour by teachers themselves.

Many teachers suggest that listening to tapes can be pleasurable and even exciting when it provides surprising insights about the ways in which pupils participate. One teacher states:

> 'I have become aware that in examining talk I have become more sensitive than formerly to the process by which children construct their meanings.'

Another teacher describes the detail which is available from listening to and transcribing talk:

> 'Transcripts showed the children to be patient, tolerant, honest, helpful, sometimes exasperated and relaxed. They were free to ask questions in a more informal atmosphere without embarrassment.
> The children were able to co-operate with each other and allowed

every group member to participate. I was especially pleased to find that the youngest child in my highlighted group was able to work so well in the group, and that the others were tolerant enough to modify their behaviour to take account of his relative immaturity. He was able to talk without any embarrassment and showed no signs of talking in a muddled or stilted way.

I was surprised to find the extent to which the children gained skills in group management. Some children adapted to working in groups more naturally than others. They had an instinctive awareness that they should sit in a friendly formation. They were able to listen to each other and take turns.'

A teacher of seven- and eight-year-olds summarises:

'By reading the transcripts and listening to the tapes I realised how much young children can do by themselves. Whilst observing, I was occasionally tempted to intervene – had I done so I would undoubtedly have changed their course. In fact, they completed the task in the way they saw fit. It is likely that they gained more from following their own course than from taking the lead from me. I hope I will be less ready to criticise what I see as irrelevant contributions or material in the future, and so give more opportunities for this kind of undirected work.

By maintaining a low profile I was hopefully encouraging the children to become self-reliant rather than teacher dependent. The children were extremely capable and mostly willing to help each other and were actively promoting each other's learning. They certainly didn't need me to answer low-level requests. The responsibility for success relied on the children participating together. With this came the realisation that my presence was not necessarily required for learning to take place.'

Concern about whether to intervene in groups is often voiced, but many teachers do decide in retrospect that there is more to be gained both socially and academically by 'standing back', even when this is not the way in which they felt they ought to behave at the time.

'When listening carefully to the tapes I could hear that I had caused the children to stop developing an argument to speak to me. I had gone to see if they needed help.'

This is particularly the case when children are not tackling the task in the ways anticipated. One teacher reports an activity with a group of reception children which turned out to be particularly rewarding in both social terms and the creative use of language. After listening to a tape she states:

'The children learned about materials, including the bowl of water, and had a lot of fun in the process. Under normal classroom conditions I may have felt it necessary to stop the children playing with the water and bring them back to what I considered the task to be. This would have greatly reduced the amount of on task talk. There must be time in my own practice when the children are allowed more freedom to talk and it must be monitored from a distance in the form of tape recording, allowing me to listen and analyse the talk more carefully, not making so many assumptions.'

Eggins *et al.* (1979) suggest that listening to audio tapes is invaluable since it 'allows the teacher to assess the standard of oral work, to check on the progress and behaviour of members of the group and thereby reassure himself about what took place in his absence.' It is this kind of reassurance that seems to convince teachers that co-operative groupwork really is worthwhile and that their own presence is not always essential. The following series of conversations reveal a number of features about the serious approach of which young children are capable, as well as insights into their feelings about co-operative work. Pupils have been recorded while evaluating their own activities.

Anthony: We got on well.

Chlöe: It was OK sometimes . . . depending what mood people were in.

Nadine: It was a good experience for Anthony being with three girls.

Anthony: I've never been on my own with three girls. It was OK. I didn't think we'd get on that well. They were very fair.

Nadine: When we discussed things, we could see more things.

Karen: Getting other people's opinions helped.

Another group of four children (two boys and two girls) demonstrate considerable change over a short period of time. At first, the two boys tend to exclude themselves, co-operate little and show little interest in the task. The girls seem frustrated.

Nicky: I don't know why we had to put industries in. It didn't seem right.

Joe: I thought it was a brochure for a holiday camp.

Alec: I think it's boring.

Nicky: You keep putting things off and Joe gets half way through.

Joe: I started something.

Nicky: You started and it took about four hours.

Joe: Two!
Nicky: And we told you to do something more worthwhile.
Joe: I like my boat.

It seems, however, that peer pressure works wonders in terms of involvement and motivation. Later in this project, the situation has clearly changed.

Nicky: Alison's done too much work at the beginning, it's all your work.
Joe: That's not fair.
Alison: It is now, because suddenly you sprang – something went 'boing' . . . and they [the boys] got going.
Joe: It took me a long time to get into it. I thought it was boring and then I started doing some work and it was really interesting. The girls helped. They said have a go – they forced me to do it. The girls seem to take charge . . .
Joe: If we work again in a group it will be even better because we know everyone's weak point.
Nicky: We can rely on them now.
Joe: You couldn't rely on us to start with.
Nicky: We know what Alec can do and if we push him a little hard we get the result we want.
Alison: It sounds like you're training a dog! We know what his work is like and how to get the best out of him.

After one piece of history work in this group, Joe, the lowest attainer said: 'I would like to go back to the 1490s knowing the knowledge I know now.'

This atypical statement so much surprised and overjoyed the teacher that it was replayed to both the class tutor and the year leader, who both expressed surprise. In this case, reassurance about the power of groupwork and the responsibility of children was certainly provided.

Our research shows that listening to tapes can also, at times, prove frustrating:

'Keeping track of how well each individual contributes during a set period of time is difficult. One feels that listening to tapes after the event, on the way home in the car or during lunch is too late, obviously, to allow intervention that can help to direct the group's efforts towards the goal. However, it may be preferable to not hearing the pupil interaction at all as might often be the case in the class.'

There is no question that the best way of monitoring participation and progress is by listening to audio recordings of group talk. Audio recording will also become an essential part of the 'evidence' needed to satisfy the demands of the National Curriculum for Speaking and Listening, along with short transcripts of talk which allow a deeper analysis. It may also provide data on 'particular words or moments which were revealing' (suggested by the Non-Statutory Guidance for Key Stage 1) over a range of activities.

Assessment of this kind only becomes problematic if teachers are faced with children who are particularly reluctant to participate in talk. This did not in fact appear in any of our research, since time and again it was found that pupils who seldom, if ever, addressed the teacher, did actually make their presence felt in a group. Over a period of time, and if groupwork gives children confidence, it seems at least possible that apparently reluctant talkers will participate more widely in classroom activities.

A few teachers reported that audio recording proved difficult, mostly because of children's interest in the procedure and because they talked to the recorder, and that listening was at times impossible due to background noise. However, it also became clear that children soon became used to the presence of a tape recorder and were quite able to use it appropriately. Pupils' involvement and interest can also be stimulated by playing back parts of a tape to the group – children often seem excited and surprised by their own contributions, and this could be important in terms of training and self-monitoring of skills.

Experimenting with the positioning of the group to be recorded will allow for the possibility of better sound; a recent technical development in the shape of a 'plate microphone' has also demonstrated itself to be particularly effective in the groupwork context.

Modes of assessment

Much of what is important in co-operative groupwork can only be assessed during the process. Audio tapes are particularly useful since they allow for a clear insight into this process, and for this reason discussion of them is included under 'monitoring'. They do, however, also allow for the assessment of that process after the event. Yet often, a teacher will need to assess groupwork after a task has been completed and will have no record of the process, either from an audio tape or from close observation. We now discuss ways in which this can be done, making a distinction between tasks which, first, have an assessable end-product and, second, do not have an assessable end-product since they are solely dependent on discussion.

Tasks with an end-product

Tasks of this nature might be: making an artefact such as a model, a piece of writing or a drawing.

When *individual end-products* are demanded by the task, even though the children are working as a group, it is clear that each child's work can be assessed individually. The only problems with the assessment of this individual work are that some pupils may copy others, or lean heavily on others' ideas without producing their own.

When *joint end-products* are demanded by the task, individual assessment is more difficult. Individual accountability is low and it is difficult for the teacher to know what each child has contributed.

There are several methods by which teachers can gain more information about the ways in which children worked at the task which will in turn inform their assessment of the end-product.

(a)   *Post-task interviews* with individuals or groups will enable teachers to ascertain the degree of participation and under-standing of each child, the nature of support to, or from, others, etc.

(b)   *Whole-class discussion* allows teachers to review a task as children report back on their activities and reflect on their work; end-products can be compared or analysed critically and pupils' responses will indicate their degree of involvement in, and understanding of, the task.

(c)   *Post-task written tests (or drawings)* demonstrate the extent to which individual children have learned or understood specific features relating to the task they have just completed. The written, or drawn, product is easily assessed.

Tasks without an end-product

Tasks without an end-product (ie, discussion tasks) are always dependent on *joint participation* in the development of ideas, the airing of opinions, the raising of arguments, and so on. Although monitoring of the process itself will always give the most information, the same methods as those given above will be appropriate for gathering feedback from the pupils as to how they tackled the task.

(a)   *Post-task interviews* with individuals, groups or the whole class.

(b)   *Whole-class discussion* where teachers can review arguments, investigate hypotheses, consider ideas and understand how conclusions were reached. In short, the children enable the teacher to take part in the process of their discussions, but retrospectively.

(c)   *Post-task writing (or drawing).* The discussion task may be followed up by a piece of writing or a drawing: an end-product produced either individually or jointly. Often this is integral to the task and assessed in its own right.

Below are presented some teachers' accounts to illustrate(a)–(c) above.

(a) Post-task interviews. Interviews with children after completing their tasks can take different forms and are used for different purposes. This is shown below by the ways in which two different teachers talk to their children.

A teacher who asked groups of six- and seven-year-olds to build a shelter out of Quadro deliberately did not involve herself with the children during the task. Her interviews, however, demonstrate to them that she is interested in their groups and what they have done, as well as telling her about the level of participation of each child and whether they were satisfied with the group's end-product.

These were actually individual interviews, but similar questions would be appropriate for groups or even a class.

Teacher:	You all made a lovely house today. Which parts of it did you build?
Sarah:	Well I decided to build in the ladder and two windows. I helped Leanne to build the windows, and I helped with the little square that we did first.
Gemma:	I did a couple of the top bits. I did some of the starting bit where you make it up and the bottom bit and some of the side bit.
Teacher:	If you could go and spend longer on it would you make any changes to it?
Anthony:	Yes. Well that straight bit, you know when Benjamin had that long bit where two bits went in, and I said 'Ben I don't think that will work,' because there wasn't a bit like it on the other side, well I would change that bit.
Benjamin:	Well, I'd just make it look a bit, a lot better.
Teacher:	How would you do that?
Benjamin:	Well, so, just. Just imagine that Robinson Crusoe had to stay in it for a night, right, well I'd make it longer. I'd make the sides longer and I'd make it a bit taller.

In post-task interviews it is also possible to assess progress and learning. With older children (ten-year-olds), a teacher interviews a group about a poem they have been reading and illustrating by themselves, so that he can check for their attempts at meaning-making and understanding. The task had been set as a co-operative problem-solving activity and this interview demonstrates the continuation of a sharing process with the pupils themselves taking on a questioning role and the teacher's presence barely necessary, except to confirm his interest in the children. He is thus able to concentrate fully on the talk, their reaching for meaning and the understanding which they relate to their own personal experiences. Part of the interview is given below:

Discussion of 'The Forest of Tangle'

Teacher:	Did you enjoy the poem? [Pause]
Samantha:	I like it, he sounds like a nice man.
Mary Anne:	So do I, he likes animals and he lives with them so that he can make them better.
Matthew:	He's on his own, he's lonely.
Mary Anne:	He's got the animals but he cried – he was crying because he was on his own.
Neil:	He's the King . . . [Pause] Kings are lonely.
Teacher:	What do you think he was doing?
Matthew:	Crying – he was crying. [Indistinct, several voices]
Mary Anne:	He was alone and he helped the animals in the forest, he had lots of things for them, to help them.
Samantha:	He didn't sell them because no one came, he was like a . . . maker who can't sell what he makes.
Mary Anne:	He made things for people but they didn't come, he made all sorts of things.
Matthew:	He made animals with the bits, he was making animals from all the different parts.
Neil:	Is he a god? Is the King of the makers a god?
Mary Anne:	He is sort of . . . like that because he made lots of things.
Samantha:	If he is a god why does he cry, why is he crying?
Matthew:	Because . . .
Neil:	I know . . .
Matthew:	Because he's making . . . [Pause]
Mary Anne:	He's making the world and he doesn't know why.

(b) **Whole class discussion.** A teacher explains how she brought the class together at the end of each co-operative groupwork class. Her pupils were aged between six and eight, but this form of organisation lends itself to children of any age.

> 'I deliberately designed the tasks so that there was no obvious solution for each problem. There was never an occasion when each group came to the same decision. This, I believe, shows that the problems were open-ended. It also meant that the class discussion after each session was broad and lively.
>
> After each groupwork task, the whole class came together to talk about their solutions to the problems. On each occasion I asked for a quiet or low ability child from each group to explain their group decision. They were always able to do so. This showed that in each group the children were able to explain the decision the group had come to, they were therefore all involved in the learning in each task.'

It is interesting that in both post-task interviews and class follow-up periods there is some evidence of teachers promoting talk particularly in terms of abstract ideas, taking up decisions made by children and questioning and challenging. For example, those children who had been making carts with wheels and bodies of different shapes and sizes were fully aware of the proportions of their own group's product. The teacher-led discussion as to why some carts rolled further or faster than others now became meaningful to every child as they realised exactly how their own group's cart was different from another's; pupils were prepared to argue the strengths and weaknesses of their own cart.

The prospect of achieving greater understanding in children through assessment procedures is an interesting and, potentially, very fruitful one.

(c) **Post-task written tests (or drawings).** Several teachers gave their groups both pre-task and post-task written tests. An example is given below. The task which had been set for the groups was purely practical in that it demanded making cubes, but their teachers wanted to know about the knowledge of cubes these children possessed before the task and the extent to which a practical activity might extend this knowledge. One teacher reports:

> 'The group seem to have had a fairly accurate idea of objects they thought were cubes before the task. All except one child thought the faces of a cube are the same in the pre-task test. She had changed this assumption by the post-task test and she too agreed that all the faces

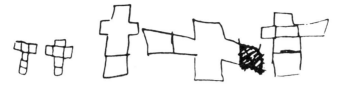

Figure 8.1 Post-task nets of cubes

of a cube are the same. None attempted to draw a net before the task in the pre-task test, but all produced fairly accurate ideas on the net of a cube in the post-task test. These are the nets they produced [Figure 8.1].'

From these nets, the teacher is able to ascertain both the children's progress and understanding, and also that the task set achieved what she had intended, that is, that the children should be able to draw nets of cubes.

Of further interest is that the knowledge gained from this task was transferred by each of the children to a new, though similar, situation – that is, the devising of nets for triangular prisms. Whereas in the first pre-task test no child was able to attempt a net of a cube, each tried to do so for the triangular prisms (Figure 8.2). Although these attempts are not accurate, they do all represent specific features that are essential to such prisms; after working together to construct prisms, each individual is then able to draw an accurate net and this final product is available for teacher assessment (Figure 8.3).

By means of a written test, it is also possible to provide an assessment picture over a longer period of time. One teacher used a simple written

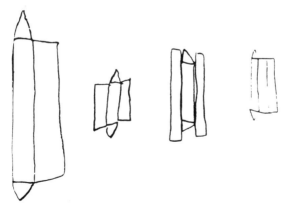

Figure 8.2 Pre-task nets of triangular prisms

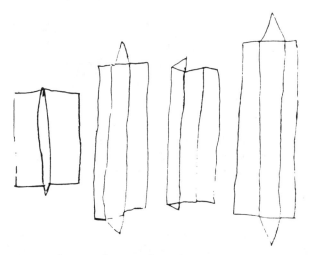

Figure 8.3 Post-task nets of triangular prisms

Questions on task sheets	Pre-task				Post-task (same day)				Post-task (one week later)				Post-task (two weeks later)			
	Hi	Av	Av	Low	Hi	Av	Av	Low	Hi	Av	Av	Low	Hi	Av	Av	Low
Draw two dice.	✓	✓	✓	✗	✓	✓	✓	✗	✓	✓	✓	✓	✓	✓	✓	✓
What shape is a die?	✗	✗	✗	✗	✓	✓	✗	✗	✓	✓	✓	✗	✓	✓	✓	✗
How many faces has a die?	✗	✓	✗	✗	✓	✓	✗	✓	✓	✓	✓	✓	✓	✓	✓	✓
How many edges has a die?	✗	✗	✗	✗	✓	✗	✗	✗	✓	✗	✓	✗	✓	✗	✓	✗
How many vertices has a die?	✗	✗	✓	✗	✓	✓	✓	✓	✓	✓	✓	✓	✓	✓	✓	✓

Figure 8.4 Pre- and post-task knowledge about dice

activity as a pre-test before a co-operative task investigating dice. This written activity was repeated immediately after the groupwork session, then a week later and, finally, two weeks after the original attempt. The chart in Figure 8.4 shows the questions asked and the responses from a group of four pupils (one high attainer, two average and one low). The arrows show the point at which children change from an incorrect response to a correct one.

This chart not only shows that children develop understanding or knowledge at different times over this period (during which time the teacher continued work on three-dimensional shapes), but also, for these questions at least, that knowledge once gained was not forgotten. It also makes clear to the teacher that the low attainer and one of the average attainers still have problems; this clarifies for her which children need further and more individual help.

Summary

Assessment of groupwork can be achieved through monitoring of group processes, either by direct observation or by using tape-recorded evidence; the latter, we feel, is by far the most effective way to gain depth of understanding about how individuals contribute to and gain from group activities.

It is also possible to assess the process as well as the product after the group task has been completed. Tasks with an end-product provide evidence of individual and group efforts; discussion tasks can also do so during feedback to the rest of the class, during post-task interviews with the group as a whole or with individuals, or by means of post-task tests.

Assessment of groupwork is particularly difficult because of the interweaving of both social and cognitive aspects of co-operative working and the complexity of relationships which may develop and lead to different kinds of interaction and learning.

9   Conclusion

We have set out in this book a clear rationale for co-operative groupwork, together with a detailed account of the outcomes of our studies and a consideration of some of the implications for effective classroom practice. Here we draw together these threads in order to present a summary and to weave a plan of classroom action. A useful framework for these purposes is the model of the teaching cycle used in Chapter one, modified for a group task, as in Figure 9.1.

The teacher's intention was for the group to work co-operatively to make a story plan, the story to be based on a beach scene. The task was presented or introduced via an actual walk on the beach where children explored its features prior to a discussion with the teacher. This discussion is continued in the group in order to develop the story plan. The teacher observes that the children work co-operatively, with Laura taking a lead and helping other members of the group. She nevertheless considers that the group process could have been improved by building more on each other's ideas, and by encouraging all children in the group to participate. The teacher's observations and assessments led her to the decision that the task had been appropriate, but that she must consider ways of improving the manner in which the group works together.

Utilised in this way, the model is a valuable *aide memoire* for the teacher and, used over time, can give a clear picture of progress in terms of group functioning.

In the following, each element of the model is considered in turn, leading, in each case, to a set of 'action questions' designed to guide the teacher through the decision points necessary to setting up and implementing effective co-operative groups.

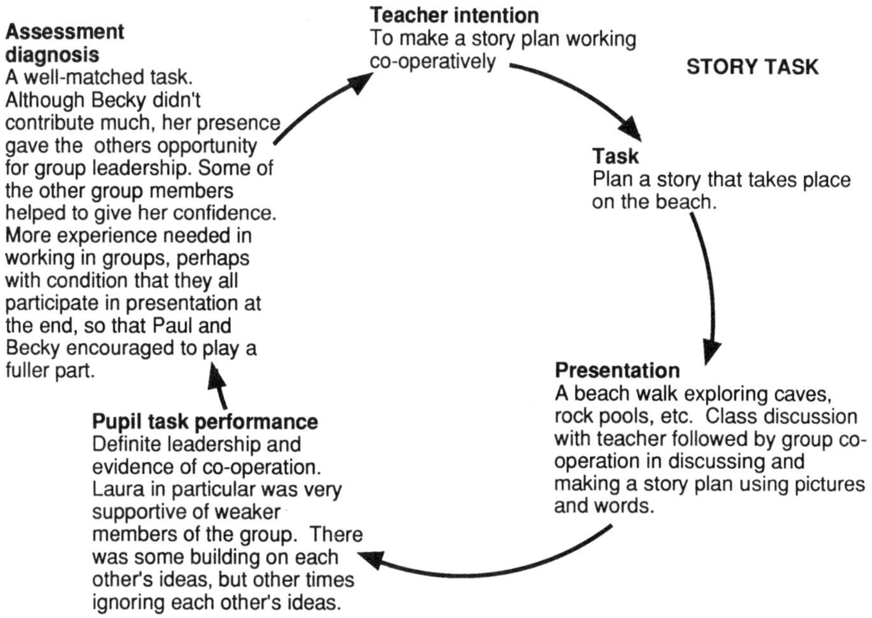
Teacher intention
To make a story plan working co-operatively
STORY TASK
Task
Plan a story that takes place on the beach.
Presentation
A beach walk exploring caves, rock pools, etc. Class discussion with teacher followed by group co-operation in discussing and making a story plan using pictures and words.
Pupil task performance
Definite leadership and evidence of co-operation. Laura in particular was very supportive of weaker members of the group. There was some building on each other's ideas, but other times ignoring each other's ideas.
Assessment diagnosis
A well-matched task. Although Becky didn't contribute much, her presence gave the others opportunity for group leadership. Some of the other group members helped to give her confidence. More experience needed in working in groups, perhaps with condition that they all participate in presentation at the end, so that Paul and Becky encouraged to play a fuller part.

Figure 9.1 A teaching cycle for a group task

Teacher intentions

Transforming intentions into appropriate tasks requires consideration of:

(a) the interaction between social and cognitive intentions;
(b) the type of task required;
(c) the match or appropriateness of the task to children in the group.

Whether the teacher's planning starts with curriculum content or with a single, or a group of, attainment targets, it is necessary to distinguish between the social and cognitive demands of the tasks. The cognitive demand relates to the curriculum content of the task, whereas the social demand relates to the type and amount of co-operation required and thus to decisions about the model of group to be chosen.

Action questions at this planning stage include:

- on which curriculum area are you going to base the task(s)?
- with which attainment targets are you dealing?
- with which specific statement of attainment are you concerned?
- which model of co-operative group is to be used?

With regard to the type of task planned we have argued that co-operative groupwork is not a panacea for children's social and cognitive development, it is one option or approach in the teacher's repertoire which must sit alongside other approaches such as individual and whole-class work. We believe it has particular value in problem-solving and applications work. It is in such types of task that abstract talk ought perhaps to predominate, if the task is designed well. However, it is worth recalling that virtually no abstract talk was apparent in the maths, science and technology tasks we observed and recorded. This does not mean that the nature of these curriculum areas precludes abstract talk; it is an issue of task design. There is thus a major challenge for teachers to develop tasks in these curriculum areas that incorporate demands for abstract talk and thought.

Our findings in this area support those of Margaret Donaldson (1978) who found that abstract talk is more difficult for children to generate, and is less fluent than talk relating to action. Teachers need to be aware of this since early attempts at abstract talk may be hesitant and less coherent. It should, nevertheless, be encouraged.

Action questions here are:

- what kind of task is required to fulfil your intention – problem-solving, discussion, production?
- will your demand be 'tight' or 'loose'?
- will this task generate the kind of talk you desire?

The third aspect of transforming intentions into tasks is the 'match' or appropriateness of task demands to children's capabilities. Typically, the concept of matching has focussed on the individual child and the extent to which tasks have been matched to that child's ability, or have overestimated or underestimated it. However, Vygotsky's notion of the zone of proximal development shifts the focus to the individual child acting in co-operation with others (Vygotsky, 1962). In this context, match is achieved by the mediation of others through the medium of talk. This shift in focus has implications for the teacher's role. No longer does it become necessary to fine-tune matching; matching can be considered more broadly, as long as the task is appropriate for co-operative groupwork. In these circumstances, matching will be achieved when children in the group make sense of task demands through their talk. As we have seen in this study, and as has been reported elsewhere, it can occur to the benefit of all children irrespective of their level of attainment.

Action questions of relevance here are:

- what is the actual task chosen?
- is it suitable for co-operative working?
- does it fit the group model chosen?
- are the cognitive demands reasonably appropriate to the children's capabilities?

Presentation and implementation

These two aspects of the model are considered together since decisions about presentation (eg, whether to introduce a task by means of a walk on the beach, or a discussion, or a television programme, etc) are closely tied up with the way in which the class and the groups are managed and supported. They have common implications for the teacher's role.

Foremost among these is the nature of the teacher's own language. As HMI (1989b) recently argued in their report on primary maths, 'It was the quality of the exposition and dialogue with the teacher that enabled the children to reflect upon and think through mathematical problems and ideas. This factor, more than any other, marked the difference between good and mediocre work.'

Of particular relevance to groupwork has been the continuing debate about the extent and nature of teacher intervention with groups. Some researchers and commentators feel that the teacher ought to operate a 'hands-off' approach, whereas others argue the opposite. The National Oracy Project has, for example, recently argued (NOP, 1990) that one of the major roles for teachers is to model effective and supportive use of talk in their own behaviour. With specific regard to groupwork they argue that it is better to be involved fully with one group than try to spend a few minutes with each. This is the best way to create planned intervention that may extend children's thinking, to introduce a new aspect, or to give the teacher more information about individuals, while the other groups are responsible for their own success. Joining in activities, they argue, rather than supervising them, extends the possibilities for dialogue.

Although published in 1990 the above recommendations clearly have their genesis in the Bullock Report published fifteen years earlier. It set out its advice as follows:

'The teacher's role should be one of planned intervention, and his purposes and the means of fulfilling them must be clear in his mind. Important among these purposes should be the intention to increase the complexity of the child's thinking, so that he does not rest on the mere expression of opinion but uses language in an exploratory way. The child should be encouraged to ask good questions as well as provide answers, to set up hypotheses and test them, and to develop the habit of trying out alternative explanations instead of being satisfied with one . . .

It is important that the teacher should spend time with each of the small groups to guide the language into fulfilling its purpose. "Guidance" is not used here in the sense of dominant intervention; indeed receptive silence is as much a part of it as the most persuasive utterance. The teacher has first to be a good listener, letting his genuine interest act as a stimulus. His questions will encourage the pupils to develop or clarify points in their thinking, or take them beyond it into the contemplation of other possibilities. We must not give the impression, however, that this is a simple matter and that there are no problems . . .

The teacher must devise situations in which the pupils will naturally adopt the kind of behaviour he wants to encourage. In other words, he must structure the learning so that the child becomes positively aware of the need for a complicated utterance, and is impelled to make it. In this way the teacher's skilled and carefully controlled intervention is a valuable means of extending his pupils' thinking and making new demands upon their language.' (10.11)

Although we respect the above advice, we have no evidence to present from our own studies to support this type of approach. We utilised a 'hands-off' study so far as teachers were concerned because of our wish to ascertain how children in groups worked without teacher input, and how they dealt with devolved responsibilities for pupil requests.

An issue linked with the National Oracy Project advice about dealing in depth with one group at a time is that of discipline and control. Losing and maintaining control are always high on the list of teacher concerns, and are certainly criteria that teachers consider when asked to change their practice. Our experience is that anxieties of this kind are unfounded, and similar findings are reported elsewhere. Cohen (1986), for example, writing from her research in American classrooms, argues:

'From the teacher's point of view, groupwork solves two common discipline problems. It helps with the problem of the low-achieving student who is often found doing anything but what he or she is supposed to be doing. Moreover, it helps to solve the problem of what the rest of the class should be doing while the teacher works intensively with one group. The most typical strategy is to have the rest of the students working with pencil and paper at their seats. However, this produces all kinds of discipline problems. If the rest of the class has been trained to work independently in groups, the teacher will be free to give direct instruction to one small group.'

The final aspect of presentation and implementation considered here is the composition of classroom groups. Our findings are clear – mixed ability groups of about four children provide a good environment for effective groupwork. Helping behaviour in the form of knowledge sharing and the provision of explanations tends not to happen in ability groups of low and average attaining children. Importantly, high attainers do not suffer in mixed ability groups. Sex differences are also apparent, and our provisional findings indicate that groups in which boys outnumber girls could depress language experience for the latter.

Questions to guide action in the area of presentation and implementation are:

- how will the task be presented/introduced?
- what expectations have you for group behaviour and co-operation? How will the children be informed?
- will the responsibility for pupil requests be devolved to the groups?
- what is your strategy for intervening in the groups?
- how will you compose your groups?

Assessment

Assessment is not a discrete teacher activity. Much of it takes place during the implementation stage, through teacher observations and questions. Assessment serves several different purposes, for which different techniques are required. Assessment of group processes, through which teachers gain understanding of the nature and quality of pupil interaction, is best achieved in our experience through the use of a tape recorder. Children soon ignore the machine even if there is some initial 'microphone talk'. Not only does the teacher gain an insight into the talk used, but also into interaction patterns, the development and changes in leadership roles and early indications of forms of group malfunctioning.

The quality of these processes will reflect in the quality of group outcomes, the assessment of which requires different techniques. We have highlighted several of these including interviewing individual, or groups of, children in order to access their understanding or schema. Short written assessments can also be used for this purpose. Class discussions can also draw out contrasts in group thinking and approaches.

Some of these techniques require time to carry out and record. Nevertheless, this is time well spent. Better understanding of children's attainment and developing schema should feed forward into better planning of future tasks.

Action questions here are:

- what are you going to assess?
- how are you going to assess it?
- how are you going to feed back to pupils and groups?
- how are you going to record your assessments?
- how are you going to use this information in planning future tasks?

School issues

The focus thus far has exclusively been on teaching and learning in the classroom. But no classroom is an island. What happens in it, or is allowed to happen in it, is markedly affected by the policies of the school and the attitudes of the head and the rest of the staff. Successive HMI reports have advocated school-based schemes, and recent research has attested to the importance of the head and deputy headteachers and their role in providing guidance for common teaching approaches as well as common curriculum schemes (Mortimore *et al.*, 1988). Where guidance is absent, or the ethos is antagonistic to change, the individual teacher who wishes to innovate can become dispirited and de-motivated due to lack of support.

Several of the teachers we have worked with have experienced such attitudes and it takes considerable strength of will and character to withstand the criticism of one's colleagues. HMI (1983) have also found it necessary to comment on this.

'Sometimes, it seemed that the teachers were worried that activities which revolved around talk or discussion would produce too little evidence of work done. Where headteachers were convinced of the value of talk as a means of making sense of experience and communicating with others and conveyed these views to their teachers the quality of discussion and of resulting written work was good.'

An approach like co-operative groupwork ideally needs a school-based commitment, otherwise children find themselves weaving from one set of classroom rules to another as they progress through the school – a sort of cultural lurch through learning contexts. The value of co-operation and talk needs to be seen as important throughout the school, otherwise there can be no planned development of experience and skill, and no perception among teachers or learners of common aims.

In developing an agreed school scheme, it is important that parents and governors be involved in the process. Parents will, for example, quite rightly want to probe into the impact of co-operative working in mixed ability groups, and teachers will need an agreed justification for their practice. The National Oracy Project, in commenting on this issue, offered the following advice (NOP, 1990).

'If talk is to be valued as a tool for learning and a means of communication of educational worth equal to reading and writing, its status may have to be improved in the eyes of everyone concerned with the children and the school.

Teachers in the Project have organized workshops for parents and attended governors' meetings to explain the emphasis being given to talking and listening. They have found that getting people to share experiences about the importance of talk in their own lives, good and bad, has been an effective way of making their point.'

Throughout this book, we have highlighted the issues involved in setting up and working with co-operative groups and have suggested conditions under which they may most effectively thrive. Changing one's classroom practice is never unproblematic, but the evidence is clear that co-operative groupwork holds the promise of improving the quality of classroom life for both teachers and learners.

Our work with teachers demonstrates the improvements that can be achieved both for their pupils and themselves. For pupils these improvements are evident in enhanced levels of involvement, in the range and nature of their talk and in the quality of their completed work; for teachers it is shown in the creation of time; time which is crucially necessary for the diagnosis, assessment and recording of children's attainments. Thus for all those who are interested in developing classroom practice, co-operative groupwork is worthy of serious consideration.

Appendix A

As indicated in Chapter 3, in order to take into account quantity and mode of talk a 'fair share' analysis is required. A fair share in a group of, for example, five children is defined as the total words spoken divided by five. A fair share index is then calculated as the percentage by which each boy or girl in the group differs from their fair share. So if more is spoken than their fair share a plus score will result, and a negative score for those who spoke less than their fair share. Examples of this can be seen in Table A.1 which shows modes of talk in language, in relation to three types of group composition (ie, when there are equal numbers of boys and girls, where there are more girls than boys and more boys than girls).

Table A.1 Modes of talk in different types of group: Language tasks

Mode of talk	Group Type					
			More girls than boys		More boys than girls	
	b	g	b	g	b	g
Non-collaborative	+19	−19	+24	−10	−8	+11
Sharing in action	−20	+20	−43	+18	+4	−7
Collaborative in abstract	−44	+44	−54	+24	+6	−10

References

Alexander R J (1984) *Primary Teaching*. London. Holt, Rinehart and Winston.

Aronson E (1978) *The Jigsaw Classroom*. Beverly Hills. Sage.

Assessment and Performance Unit (1986) *Speaking and Listening, Assessment at Age 11*. Windsor. NFER-Nelson.

Ausubel D P (1968) *Educational Psychology: A Cognitive View*. New York. Holt, Rinehart and Winston.

Bargh J A, Schul Y (1980) 'On the cognitive benefits of teaching'. *Journal of Educational Psychology*, 72, 593–604.

Barnes D, Todd F (1977) *Communication and Learning in Small Groups*. London. Routledge and Kegan Paul.

Bell B (1985) 'The construction of meaning and conceptual change in classroom settings: Case studies on plant nutrition'. *Children's Learning in Science Project*. University of Leeds.

Bennett N (1985) 'Interaction and achievement in classroom groups'. In: Bennett N, Desforges C (Eds) *Recent Advances in Classroom Research*. Monograph 2. *British Journal of Educational Psychology*. Edinburgh. Scottish Academic Press.

Bennett N (1987) 'The search for the effective primary teacher'. In: Delamont S (Ed) *The Primary School Teacher*, pp. 45–61. Lewes. Falmer Press.

Bennett N, Andreae J, Hegarty P, Wade B (1980) *Open Plan Schools*. Windsor. NFER.

Bennett N, Cass A (1988) 'The effects of group composition on group interactive processes and pupil understanding'. *British Educational Research Journal*, 15, 19–32.

Bennett N, Desforges C (1988) 'Matching classroom tasks to students' attainments'. *Elementary School Journal*, 88, 221–34.

Bennett N, Desforges C, Cockburn A, Wilkinson B (1984) *The Quality of Pupil Learning Experiences*. London. Erlbaum.

Bennett N, Kell J (1989) *A Good Start? Four Year Olds in Infant Schools*. Oxford. Blackwell.

Bennett N, Roth E, Dunne R (1987) 'Task processes in mixed and single age classes'. *Education 3–13*, 15, 43–50.

Biott C (1984) *Getting on without the Teacher*. Centre for Educational Research and Development. Sunderland Poly.

Boydell D (1975) 'Pupil behaviour in junior classrooms'. *British Journal of Educational Psychology*, 45, 122–9.

Britton J (1970) *Language and Learning* (1972 edition). Harmondsworth. Penguin Books.

Bruner J (1986) *Actual Minds, Possible Worlds*. Cambridge (MA): Harvard University Press.

Bruner J, Haste H (1987) *Making Sense*. London. Methuen.

Bullock Report (1975) *A Language for Life*. London. HMSO.

Cohen E G (1986) *Designing Groupwork: Strategies for the Heterogeneous Classroom*. New York. Teachers' College Press.

Cowie H, Rudduck J (1988) *Co-operative Group Work: An Overview*. London. B.P. Educational Service.

Damon W, Phelps E (1989) Critical distinctions among three approaches to peer education. *International Journal of Educational Research*, 13, (19), 9–19.

DES (1989a) *National Curriculum – English 5–11*. London. HMSO.

DES (1989b) *Task Group on Assessment and Testing – A Report*. London. HMSO.

Donaldson M (1978) *Children's Minds*. London. Fontana.

Dunne E, Bennett N (1990) *Talking and Learning in Groups*. London. Macmillan.

Edwards D, Mercer N (1987) *Common Knowledge: The Development of Understanding in the Classroom*. London. Methuen.

Eggins G *et al.* (1979) *Learning Through Talking 11–16*. London. Evans/Methuen Schools Council Working Paper 64.

Epstein C (1972) *Affective Subjects in the Classroom: Exploring Race, Sex and Drugs*. Scranton, Pennsylvania. Intext Educational Publishers.

Galton M, Simon B, Croll P (1980) *Inside the Primary Classroom*. London. Routledge and Kegan Paul.

Hallinan M (1984) Summary and Implications. In: Peterson P, Wilkinson L C, Hallinan M (Eds) *The Social Context of Instruction*. New York. Academic.

Harlen W (1985) *Taking the Plunge*. London. Heinemann.

Her Majesty's Inspectorate (1978) *Primary Education in England*. London. HMSO.

Her Majesty's Inspectorate (1980) *Education 5–9*. London. HMSO.
Her Majesty's Inspectorate (1982) *Education 5–9*. London. HMSO.
Her Majesty's Inspectorate (1983) *9–13 Middle Schools: An Illustrative Survey*. London. HMSO.
Her Majesty's Inspectorate (1985) *Education 8–12 in Combined and Middle Schools*. London. HMSO.
Her Majesty's Inspectorate (1988) *The New Teacher in School*. London. HMSO.
Her Majesty's Inspectorate (1989a) *Aspects of Primary Education: The Teaching of History and Geography*.
Her Majesty's Inspectorate (1989b) *Aspects of Primary Education: The Teaching of Mathematics*. London. HMSO.
Her Majesty's Inspectorate (1989c) *Aspects of Primary Education: The Teaching of Science*. London. HMSO.
Her Majesty's Inspectorate (1990) *Aspects of Primary Education: The Teaching and Learning of Language and Literacy*. London. HMSO.
Jelfs M (1982) *Manual for Action*. Action Resources Group, 13 Morrington Grove, London EC 4NS.
Jenkin F (1989) *Making Small Groups Work*. Oxford. Penguin Educational.
Johnson D W, Johnson R T (1975) *Learning Together and Alone*. Englewood Cliffs. Prentice Hall.
Johnson D W, Johnson R T (1985) 'The internal dynamics of co-operative learning groups'. In: Slavin R (Ed) *Learning to Cooperate, Cooperating to Learn*. New York. Plenum.
Johnson D W, Johnson R, Maruyama G (1983) 'Interdependence and interpersonal attraction among heterogeneous and homogeneous individuals: A theoretical formulation and a meta-analysis of the research'. *Review of Educational Research*, 53, 5–54.
Johnson D W, Maruyama G, Johnson R, Nelson D, Skon L (1981) 'Effects of co-operative, competitive, and individualistic goal structures on achievement: A meta-analysis'. *Psychological Bulletin*, 89, 47–62.
Kagan S (1985) In: Slavin R E (Ed) *Learning to Cooperate, Cooperating to Learn*. New York. Plenum.
Kagan S (1988) *Cooperative Learning: Resources for Teachers*. University of California, Riverside.
Kerry T (1983) 'Talking: the teacher's role'. In Sutton C (Ed) *Communicating in the Classroom*. London. Hodder and Stoughton.
Kerry T, Eggleston J (1988) *Topic Work in the Primary School*. London. Routledge.
Kerry T, Sands M (1982) *Handling Classroom Groups: A Teaching Skills Workbook*. Basingstoke and London. Macmillan Educational Ltd.

Lee K, Cohn J, Oakes J, Farivar S, Webb N M (1985) *Helping Behaviours Handbook*. Los Angeles. University of California.

Lemlech J K (1988) *Classroom Management*. London. Longman.

Lunzer E A, Gardner K (Eds) (1979) *The Effective Use of Reading*. London. Heinemann.

Mortimore P, Sammons P, Stoll L, Lewis D, Ecob R (1988) *School Matters*. Wells. Open Books.

National Curriculum Council (1989) *English in the National Curriculum Key Stage One*. York. NCC.

National Oracy Project (1990) *Teaching, Talking and Learning in Key Stage One*. York. NCC.

Noddings N (1985) 'Small groups as a setting for research on mathematical problem solving'. In: Silver E A (Ed) *Teaching and Learning Mathematical Problem Solving*, pp. 345–59. Hillsdale, NJ. Erlbaum.

Piaget J (1959) *The Language and Thought of the Child*. London. Routledge and Kegan Paul.

Plowden Report (1967) *Children and their Primary Schools*. London. HMSO.

PRINDEP (1990) '*Teachers and children in PNP classrooms*'. Evaluation Report 11. University of Leeds Primary Needs Independent Evaluation Project.

Reason R, Rooney S, Roffe M (1987) 'Cooperative learning in the infant school'. *Educational and Child Psychology*, 4, 40–8.

Rosen C, Rosen H (1973) *The Language of Primary School Children*. Harmondsworth. Penguin Books.

Royal Society of Arts (1983) *Education for Capability*. Occasional Paper. London. RSA.

Salomon G, Globerson T (1989) 'When teams do not function the way they ought to'. *International Journal of Educational Research*, 13, (1), 89–99.

Salter B, Tapper T (1981) *Education, Politics and the State*. London. Grant McIntyre.

Schmuck R A (1985). In: Slavin E R (Ed) *Learning to Cooperate, Cooperating to Learn*. New York. Plenum.

SEAC (1990) A Source Book of Teacher Assessment, Pack C from *A Guide to Teacher Assessment*. Heinemann Education on behalf of SEAC. London. Heinemann.

Sharan S (1980) 'Co-operative learning in small groups: recent methods and effects on achievement, attitudes and ethnic relations'. *Review of Educational Research*, 50, 241–71.

Simon S B, Howe L W, Kirschenbaum H (1972) *Values Clarification: A Handbook of Practical Strategies for Teachers and Students*. New York. Hart Publishing Co.

Slavin R E (1983) *Cooperative Learning*. New York. Longman.
Slavin R E (1987) 'Developmental and motivational perspectives on co-operative learning: A reconciliation'. *Child Development*, 58, 1161–7.
Southgate V, Arnold H, Johnson S (1981) *Extending Beginning Reading*. London. Heinemann Educational Reading Books.
Tann C S (1980) *A study of Groupwork in Primary and Lower Secondary Schools*. University of Leicester. Unpublished PhD Thesis.
Task Group on Assessment and Testing (TGAT) (1988) *National Curriculum*. Department of Education and Science. London. HMSO.
Topping K (1988) *The Peer Tutoring Handbook*. London. Croom Helm.
Tizard B, Blatchford P, Burke J, Farquhar C, Plewis I (1988) *Young Children at School in the Inner City*. London. Erlbaum.
Vygotsky L S (1962) *Thought and Language*. Cambridge; MIT Press.
Vygotsky L S (1978) *Mind in Society: The Development of Higher Psychological Processes*. Cambridge, MA. Harvard University Press.
Webb N M (1982) 'Student interaction and learning in small groups'. *Review of Educational Research*, 52, 421–45.
Webb N M (1987) *Helping Behaviour to Maximize Learning*. Los Angeles. University of California.
Webb N M (1989) 'Peer interaction and learning in small groups'. *International Journal of Educational Research*, 13, 21–39.
Webb N M, Ender P, Lewis S (1986) 'Problem-solving strategies and group processes in small groups learning computer planning'. *American Education Research Journal*, 23.
Wragg E, Bennett N, Carré C (1989) 'Primary Teachers and the National Curriculum'. *Research Papers in Education*, 4, 3.